GLORY DAYS

Tilling Group

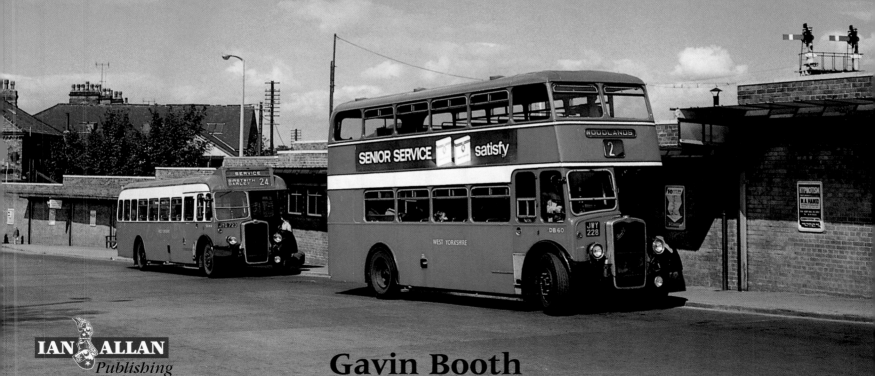

IAN ALLAN
Publishing

Gavin Booth

Front cover: Bristol/Eastern Coach Works vehicles were synonymous with the Tilling Group for its 20-year stint in state ownership. This is a 1958 Bristol LS5G with 45-seat ECW body. United Welsh No 107 (OCY 947), seen in Llanelly in July 1963. *P. R. Wallis*

Back cover: The Bristol/ECW Lodekka model was the Tilling Group's main double-deck model for more than a decade. West Yorkshire No DX62 (TWY 604), a 1958 LD6B 60-seater, at Harrogate bus station in 1965. *G. W. Dickson*

Title page: Symbolic of Tilling's high level of standardisation — Bristol K and L types with ECW bodies, in Tilling red/cream, at Harrogate bus station in August 1965. In front is No DB60 (JWY 228), a 1951 KSW6B with lowbridge 55-seat body, and behind is No SWG8, an LL5G with 39-seat bus body, new in the same year. *G. W. Dickson*

Contents

First published 1998

ISBN 0 7110 2597 5

© Ian Allan Publishing Ltd 1998

Published by Ian Allan Publishing

an imprint of Ian Allan Publishing Ltd, Terminal House, Station Approach, Shepperton, Surrey TW17 8AS.
Printed by Ian Allan Printing Ltd, Riverdene Business Park, Molesey Road, Hersham, Surrey KT12 4RG

Code: 9808/B3

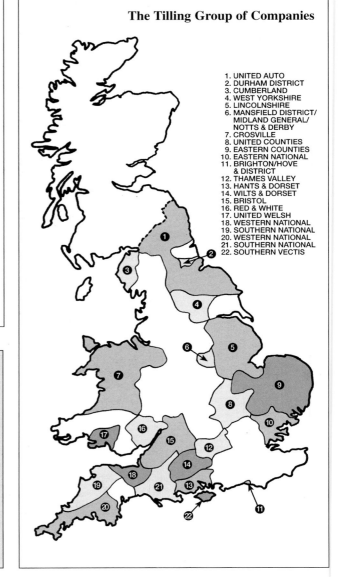

The Tilling Group of Companies

1. UNITED AUTO
2. DURHAM DISTRICT
3. CUMBERLAND
4. WEST YORKSHIRE
5. LINCOLNSHIRE
6. MANSFIELD DISTRICT/ MIDLAND GENERAL/ NOTTS & DERBY
7. CROSVILLE
8. UNITED COUNTIES
9. EASTERN COUNTIES
10. EASTERN NATIONAL
11. BRIGHTON/HOVE & DISTRICT
12. THAMES VALLEY
13. HANTS & DORSET
14. WILTS & DORSET
15. BRISTOL
16. RED & WHITE
17. UNITED WELSH
18. WESTERN NATIONAL
19. SOUTHERN NATIONAL
20. WESTERN NATIONAL
21. SOUTHERN NATIONAL
22. SOUTHERN VECTIS

Introduction

◄ The large United Automobile company, with territory stretching from East Anglia to the Scottish border, was a valuable prize around the time the railways were buying into bus companies. Crossing the causeway to Holy Island, off the Northumberland coast, in 1954 is United No BG387 (LHN 829), a 1950 standard Bristol L5G with ECW 35-seat rear entrance bus body, one of hundreds of L types in the United fleet, and one of thousands supplied to Tilling companies. A service was operated between Berwick and Holy Island, which was subject to the tide times.
Ian Allan library

For a significant part of the past 150 years the Tilling name was one of the best known in public transport, firstly as operators of horsebuses, then as motorbus pioneers, and then as a fast-growing group which formed the basis of the British Transport Commission's nationalised bus interests in England and Wales.

This book is concerned with Tilling's years as a public corporation, from 1948 to 1968, when it operated around 10,000 buses through its patchwork quilt of subsidiary companies. The Tilling Group believed in public service, and its senior executives sought and achieved a remarkably high degree of standardisation among its companies, a principle which was adopted by its 1969 successor, the National Bus Company.

The fact that two Tilling companies — Bristol Tramways and Eastern Counties — had started building bus chassis and bodies for their own use meant that the Group had in-house manufacturing capacity that would increasingly be used for the Group fleets. After nationalisation in 1948, only state-owned undertakings could buy Bristol chassis and Eastern Coach Works bodies, and this had great benefits for Tilling companies in particular, which built up substantial fleets of efficient, well-built buses and coaches.

A look at the map suggests that Tilling got the poorer deal in the division of companies between Tilling and the BET Group in 1942, yet the Group as a whole was consistently profitable, in spite of passenger figures that dropped by a quarter between the peak year of 1955 and the setting up of the National Bus Company in 1969.

This book offers a portrait of an organisation that played an important part in urban and rural life in the 1950s and 1960s, carrying an average of over 4.3 million passengers every day at its peak.

Gavin Booth
Edinburgh

The Bristol K quickly became the Tilling Group's standard double-deck model. This is Thames Valley No 497 (EJB 219), a 1948 K6B model, with Bristol AVW engine, and lowbridge 55-seat ECW body. It is seen at Reading General station in 1963, with an Aldershot & District AEC Reliance/Weymann and a Smiths of Reading Bedford SB/Duple Vega in the background. *P. R. Wallis*

United Counties was one of the small group of companies owned by Tilling rather than Tilling & BAT. This late-model Bristol KSW6B with 55-seat ECW lowbridge body, No 931 (JBD 968), was new in 1954. The extra length and width of the 27ft x 8ft KSW type is evident when compared with the 26ft x 7ft 6in Thames Valley K type in the previous photo. *R. L. Wilson*

1. From Jobmaster to State Corporation

Thomas Tilling moved to London in 1847 and set up in business as a jobmaster, supplying horses for a wide range of transport work, but he quickly recognised the business opportunities presented by horse buses, still a relatively recent phenomenon, and in 1850 he started operating between Peckham and Oxford Street. The Tilling horsebuses were well organised and the business grew from its South London base. A public company, Thomas Tilling Ltd was formed in 1897 by two of Thomas's 11 children, his sons Richard and Edward.

The early years of the 20th century saw the birth of the motorbus, and the various London horse bus operators recognised a need to acknowledge this noisy and often unreliable newcomer, and hedge their bets by buying some. Tilling chose the Milnes-Daimler, which undoubtedly turned out to be the best of the early motorbuses, but all was not plain sailing, and while many pioneering motorbus operators went out of business in these early days, the broader base of the Tilling business helped it to survive.

By 1908 it was clear that the motorbus was here to stay, in London at least, and that year three of the biggest operators merged under the London General Omnibus Company (LGOC) name to cut their losses through co-operation and standardisation. Tilling stayed out of the new combine, but entered a pooling agreement with LGOC in 1909, which helped to protect its South London fastness.

Three years later Tilling moved closer to LGOC, but while this protected Tilling's position in London, it restricted its fleet there to 150 buses, so Tilling turned its eyes to the rest of the country, where motorbus development was more patchy.

Red & White's Newbury & District company was transferred to Thames Valley after the Red & White group sold out to BTC. Still legally owned by Newbury & District, Thames Valley No 171 (FMO 516), a 1950 Guy Arab III with Duple lowbridge 53-seat bodywork, is seen at Newbury in July 1963. *P. R. Wallis*

Another Red & White subsidiary was Venture, Basingstoke, which was transferred to Tilling's Wilts & Dorset company. No 483 (FOT 204), a 1947 AEC Regal II with Duple 35-seat body, was one of a number of AECs which found their way into the W&D fleet, which had previously been a Leyland stronghold. *Arnold Richardson/Photobus*

One of Tilling's most significant purchases in the 1930s was National Omnibus & Transport, with the railway interests represented in the titles of its three bus-operating companies: Eastern National, Southern National and Western National. At Kingsbury Square, Aylesbury, on the service to Bedford in the early postwar years is Eastern National No 3755 (GNO 699), a 1938 Bristol K5G with ECW lowbridge bodywork of the type supplied to several Tilling fleets in the immediate prewar period. In Tilling-associated fleets the Bristol/ECW combination was already well established prior to nationalisation. The Eastern National services in this area passed, more logically, to United Counties in 1951. *C. R. L. Coles*

Around this time similar seeds were being sown by another pioneering group, which in later years would, with Tilling, control most major bus companies in England and Wales. British Electric Traction Co Ltd (BET) was, as its title suggests, involved in developing electric tramways, but quickly recognised the importance of motorbuses, initially as feeders to its tram services, but soon separate bus developments were taking place.

BET had formed a new subsidiary, British Automobile Development Co Ltd (BAD), to sponsor its bus interests, but this was quickly renamed The British Automobile Traction Co, with the rather more acceptable initials BAT. Like Tilling, BAT was involved in London, first with tramways and then with a substantial fleet of Daimler buses; again agreement was reached with the all-powerful LGOC and BET accepted a limit on the number of buses it ran in London.

So Tilling and BAT were both looking for expansion opportunities and both turned their attention to Kent. After an unsuccessful venture in Birmingham, BET had set up a motorbus operation in Deal in 1908. Tilling set up the Folkestone District Road Car Co in 1914, and two years later the BAT and Tilling interests were combined as the jointly owned East Kent Road Car Company.

Along the south coast in Sussex, where the two nascent groups found themselves in competition, acquisitions and agreements resulted in Tilling operating in Brighton and Hove, and BAT creating Southdown Motor Services.

Tilling started to look beyond southeast England and in the 1920s, working closely with BAT, in which it had a substantial holding, acquired and developed companies to lay the foundations for the area agreement companies that were

familiar for several decades and even today tend to define company boundaries.

A new company was created in 1928, Tilling & British Automobile Traction Ltd (T&BAT), formalising the existing agreements. This gave Tilling a wider range of bus company interests, but it still retained direct control of its London and Brighton operations, and BET held on to direct ownership of some of its bus companies.

A third group that played its part in the growth of Tilling was the National Omnibus & Transport Co Ltd (NO&T) which had started as an operator of steam buses in London, but had agreed with LGOC to concentrate on developments outside the metropolis. National had operations in Bedford and Essex and soon became the principal operator in much of the West Country.

The four main-line railways were watching the spread of bus services with some concern. The railway companies, particularly the Great Western Railway (GWR), already ran bus services, but in 1928 they sought to formalise the situation by obtaining parliamentary powers to operate passenger and goods vehicles. These powers were granted and the railway companies chose to buy into existing bus companies. They opened talks with T&BAT, but these dragged on and there was evidence that the railway companies might still choose to go it alone. The London Midland & Scottish Railway Company (LMS) bought the Crosville bus company in 1929, GWR bought Bristol Tramways in 1930, and LMS and the London & North Eastern Railway (LNER) had formed joint operating committees with several of the Yorkshire municipal undertakings.

DRINKA PINTA MILKA DAY

BRANKSOME CHINE
CANFORD CLIFFS 6

BOURNEMOUTH

HANTS & DORSET

◀◀ Red & White formed United
Welsh in 1938 to bring
together a number of
operators in the Swansea
area. In Neath in August
1963 is No 132 (140 ACY), a
1961 Bristol MW6G with
45-seat ECW bus body.
P. R. Wallis

◀ At a time of vehicle
shortages, Tilling companies
found non-standard buses
being drafted into their fleets.
Hants & Dorset No 1215
(JEL 754) was one of six
AEC Regent III with 53-seat
lowbridge Northern Counties
bodies which joined the
H&D fleet in 1948; they had
originally been intended for
Western SMT.
A. J. Douglas/Photobus

The mass 2pm departure was a famous feature of Red & White's Cheltenham coach station. In this May 1957 photo, Red & White No UC254 (MAX 132), a 1954 Bristol LS6G with ECW 39-seat coach body in an unusual livery application for this body style, heads for Uxbridge after the interchange between coaches had been completed. Red & White was one of the founding companies of Associated Motorways, formed in 1934 to pool the growing long-distance coach operations of various operators, including Tilling's United Counties. Bristol Tramways and Royal Blue (Western/Southern National) joined later. Associated Motorways operated a network of services stretching from the Midlands through southwest England and South Wales to the south coast and West Country.
John Aldridge

The railways were also in discussions with NO&T, which operated in the areas of all four main-line companies, and this led to a set of company names being registered, reflecting the railway companies (Eastern, Midland, Northern, Southern and Western) and ending with the title National Omnibus Co Ltd. In practice only Eastern National, Southern National and Western National actually functioned as bus companies.

T&BAT eventually forced the railway companies into a corner and agreement was reached whereby the appropriate main-line companies held a share equal to that of T&BAT. This introduced a degree of stability into the growing bus industry and allowed substantial capital investment to be made in the bus companies. Further stability followed soon with the 1930 Road Traffic Act, which introduced regulation to the industry, and controls on routes, vehicles and staff where previously such legislation, if it existed at all, was largely a local matter. The 1930 Act introduced nationwide standards, and by largely eliminating wasteful competition it gave the area agreement companies virtual monopolies, a situation that was further guaranteed by a spate of takeovers right through the 1930s when large numbers of private operators were bought out to allow further expansion.

The Tilling operations in Brighton and London were still separate from the T&BAT grouping, and Tilling went on to buy other companies directly. National Omnibus & Transport went to Thomas Tilling Ltd in 1931, and Bristol Tramways was put under Western National control. Tilling also bought United Counties, in 1931.

The creation of the London Passenger Transport Board as a public authority in 1933 affected Tilling, whose South London services were compulsorily acquired, and T&BAT, whose subsidiaries operated on the fringes of the designated London Transport area.

T&BAT prospered in the 1930s, but the relationship between the Tilling and BET factions was not always a happy one, and in 1942, when World War 2 was in its darkest days, T&BAT was wound up and its interests were divided between two new companies, Tilling Motor Services Ltd and BET Omnibus Services Ltd. In most cases the subsidiary companies were allocated to the obvious master, but there were some interesting exchanges.

Tilling took Caledonian, Crosville, Cumberland, Eastern Counties, Hants & Dorset, Lincolnshire, Southern Vectis, Thames Valley, United Auto, West Yorkshire and Wilts &

Dorset. Of these, Crosville, Cumberland and Lincolnshire had been BET companies.

BET took Aldershot & District, East Kent, East Midland, East Yorkshire, Maidstone & District, North Western, Ribble, Southdown, Trent and Yorkshire Traction. Of these, East Midland and North Western had been Tilling companies.

The split gave Tilling operating companies in southwest Scotland, northwest England, Cheshire and North Wales, south central England including the Isle of Wight, East Anglia and Lincolnshire, West Yorkshire and a substantial part of northeast England. Although most companies included a proportion of high-frequency urban work, most Tilling Motor Services territory was rural, with long inter-urban bus routes as the group's staple product. It was surprising, then, that East Midland and North Western, with more urban operations, were given to BET in exchange for Crosville, Cumberland and Lincolnshire.

The group also included its Thomas Tilling Ltd-owned companies — Brighton, Hove & District, Bristol Tramways, Eastern National, Southern National, United Counties, Westcliff-on-Sea and Western National — where the mix of operations was in some cases less rural.

World War 2 placed great demands on bus companies in Britain, and rural companies often found themselves faced with tremendous growth in demand for their services as the armed forces created camps and other installations in quieter parts of the country, and factories producing war materials were set up.

The superhuman efforts of the bus industry during the war left it exhausted in 1945. Restrictions on new bus building during the war years meant that most fleets were running with hopelessly outmoded and unsuitable vehicles, just when the public was beginning to make the most of its new freedoms and spend its money on travel. Even in the early postwar period buses were difficult to come by, as manufacturers were being encouraged to export, to help the economy. There was no shortage of bodybuilders anxious to cash in on these shortages, but unsuitable materials and lack of experience often meant that the bodies were not as good as the best prewar examples.

Britain had changed too. The country was tired and battered after six years of war, and the social uncertainty of these austerity days was reflected in the dramatic 1945 election which put the Labour Party in power. Labour quickly announced its intention to nationalise many of the service industries, including electricity and sections of the transport industry. The railways and the road haulage companies appeared to be the main targets when the 1947 Transport Act was published, but the new British Transport Commission (BTC) was given powers which left the door open for bus operation outside London at some future stage; responsibility for London Transport was passed to BTC.

Of course when BTC started to function in January 1948 it already owned a large part of the bus industry through the railway shareholdings in the territorial companies. By September that year Tilling's transport interests had been sold to BTC for £24.8 million.

This decision left BET in a difficult position. With the railway nationalisation BTC held a significant proportion of shares in the BET bus companies, and it seems likely that BTC hoped to attract BET into the fold. BET was a vociferous opponent of nationalisation, and held out until the major industry changes of 1967 finally resulted in sale to the state.

The Tilling Group was about to learn about bus operation under state control.

▼ The Tilling name survived on the coaches of Tillings Transport (BTC) Ltd which was formed after nationalisation to continue the Tilling London-based coach operation. Administrative control and vehicle maintenance were handled by the Eastern National company. At the Royal Albion Hotel, Brighton, is LYM 730, one of the batch of five 1951 AEC Regal IVs with the same distinctive style of ECW coach body that was supplied to London Transport on similar chassis the same year, forming its RFW class. *Gordon Turner/Photobus*

Advance orders meant that the Cumberland fleet continued to place new Leylands in service well into the nationalised era. Some were 'pure' Leylands, but No 150 (LAO 144), a 1952 Royal Tiger PSU1/13, was a compromise, as it carries ECW 45-seat bodywork. *Arnold Richardson/Photobus*

Another fleet of non-standard types came with the Balfour Beatty companies, which favoured AECs. Notts & Derby No 315 (JVO 941), a 1948 Regent III with Weymann 56-seat body, in pristine condition in Ilkeston garage yard in June 1965. *G. W. Dickson*

Much of the territory left in Tilling Group hands after the 1942 split-up with BET was rural, with a high proportion of long interurban services, often using double-deckers. Thames Valley No 528 (FBL 30), a 1950 Bristol K6B with ECW 55-seat lowbridge body, in West Wycombe in the early postwar period.
C. R. L. Coles

2. State Ownership

At one time it looked as if the nationalisation of the Tilling Group was just a start, and that the Labour party would not rest until all public transport was in state hands. The spectre of compulsory purchase hung over the bus industry.

After all, the British road haulage industry, apart from own-account operators, had been acquired and placed under the control of British Road Services. And there was talk of area schemes that might do the same for bus operators on a regional basis. Details were released of the Northern Passenger Road Transport Board, covering what was called the Northern Area, essentially all of Northumberland and County Durham, and a substantial chunk of North Yorkshire. Over 4,000 buses and coaches operated in that area, owned by Tilling's United Auto company, BET's Northern General group, municipalities at Darlington, Hartlepool, Middlesbrough, Newcastle, South Shields, Stockton, Sunderland, Teesside and West Hartlepool, and a large number of independents of all sizes.

The scheme, and others proposed for East Anglia and southwest England, would have had far-reaching effects on the development of road transport in Britain, particularly if they had been extended to cover the whole country. There was strong opposition to the plans, but a change of government intervened and the idea was quickly dropped.

Passengers on Tilling Group services would be largely unaware that their local bus company was now state-owned. The buses continued to look much the same as they always had done, and there was little sign of co-ordination between the Tilling companies and their new stablemate, British Railways (BR). It was the railway that seemed to give BTC most heartaches during its 14-year existence. BTC annual reports are heavy on the problems faced by BR, and sometimes seem to barely mention the Tilling Group, which probably suited the Tilling managers as it allowed them to keep their heads down and run the business as they always had done.

And there is broad agreement that Tilling ran a good organisation. Its chief officers believed in central control and imposed a high degree of standardisation on its companies. And though some companies expressed their independence in various ways, the Tilling Group presented a remarkably unified front to the world.

An impressive degree of vehicle standardisation was achieved, thanks to the group's inheritance of two major suppliers, Bristol and Eastern Coach Works (ECW). Working jointly, Bristol and ECW produced a string of buses and coaches tailored to the varied needs of the Tilling Group, and while many were solid, reliable and rather traditional vehicles, others were ground-breaking in their design concepts, and set standards the rest of the industry strove to achieve.

The Bristol Tramways & Carriage Company (BTCC) had started building buses for its own use in 1908, and in its Motor Constructional Works at Brislington it built buses for its own use and, from the 1920s, for other companies. The Great Western Railway had bought shares in BTCC in 1929, and as GWR also had an interest in the National Omnibus & Transport Company the Bristol company found itself in 1931 under Western National control. Thomas Tilling Ltd had bought a controlling interest in NO&T earlier in 1931, so Bristol became an associate company of Tilling.

The Tilling companies, many of which had no experience of Bristol chassis, continued to buy other chassis types for some time, but gradually the Bristol influence spread, and by the end of the 1930s Bristol chassis were becoming well established in Tilling fleets, as well as in unconnected fleets throughout Britain.

▼ One of the interesting early consequences of the creation of the British Transport Commission was the loan to fellow BTC subsidiary, London Transport, of 180 new Bristol K types from 1948 to cover temporary vehicle shortages. The use of side-gangway lowbridge buses was not popular with passengers used to the highbridge layout, but the buses were welcome at this difficult time. New Bristol K5G LHN 307, with typical ECW 55-seat lowbridge body, was destined to become United Auto No BGL64. London Transport roundels were normally fitted to the radiators of these buses, though this may be obscured by the radiator blind. The 'lazy' destination indicators were produced to fit the standard Tilling apertures. *John Aldridge collection*

Hants & Dorset also received some of the Leyland Titan PD1As with ECW 55-seat lowbridge bodies bought by Tilling in the early postwar years. At Winchester in April 1963 is No 1149 (GLJ 961), new in 1947. *P. R. Wallis*

Tilling group companies were often able to help each other out with vehicle loans, though United Auto No BL45 (445 LHN), a 1959 Bristol Lodekka LD6B with 60-seat ECW body, has travelled fairly far to work for Crosville at Birkenhead Woodside in May 1960. *R. L. Wilson*

ECW was descended from United Automobile Services, which was set up in the Lowestoft area in 1912 and within 20 years had spread to become a significant operator, with services stretching from East Anglia to the Scottish border. United was acquired by T&BAT and LNER in 1929 and two years later the vast area was split to leave United with a significant presence in the northeast of England, and a new company, Eastern Counties, looking after the East Anglia area.

United had built bodywork for its own fleet at Lowestoft from 1919, and these activities passed to the new Eastern Counties company. For a while Eastern Counties only built bodywork for T&BAT fleets, but in 1936 the coachbuilding side was renamed Eastern Coach Works Ltd, still under Eastern Counties control, and the new company actively sought business from companies outside the group, although inevitably group fleets represented a high proportion of its output, and increasingly Bristol chassis figured in orders. As Bristol was a Tilling, rather than a T&BAT company, the influence was strongest among the 'pure' Tilling fleets.

Now in 1948 Bristol and ECW were part of the new BTC and were prevented from selling to organisations outside the state-owned sector. In theory this meant that the Tilling and

Scottish groups, and London Transport, were its main potential customers. In practice, the vast majority of deliveries to Tilling companies came from Bristol and ECW; the Scottish group — never keen to be forced into anything — bought Bristol and ECW products as well as chassis and bodies available on the open market; and London Transport stuck to its traditional suppliers, but took 84 bodies on small Guy chassis and one on a prototype Routemaster. Bristol also turned its hand to truck chassis for British Road Services companies.

BTC was active on the acquisition trail in its early days, snapping up the substantial private group, Red & White, in February 1950. At the time the Red & White group operated around 750 buses through its two main companies, Red & White and United Welsh, and smaller subsidiaries Cheltenham District, Newbury & District, South Midland and Venture (Basingstoke). Cheltenham District was placed under Bristol Tramways control, South Midland and Newbury & District went to Thames Valley, and Venture to Wilts & Dorset.

Hicks Bros of Braintree was also bought in 1950, and was placed under Eastern National management. Later the same year three major independents in County Durham — Darlington Triumph, Express Omnibus and ABC Motor

Services — were bought and merged to form a new company, Durham District Services. It might have seemed more sensible to place the acquired companies directly under United Auto control, but as many of the services they operated lay within the territory of BET's Northern General group, the creation of a new company — admittedly a United subsidiary — prevented any division of services under the United/Northern operating agreement.

There were adjustments to areas to achieve more sensible and economic working. Eastern National's Midland area passed to United Counties in 1951, and United Counties' Oxford garage, local excursions and London express service went to South Midland.

In 1951 several of Eastern National's services in the Grays area of Essex were transferred to London Transport. The same year the isolated Stroud routes of Western National passed to Bristol Tramways, along with services developed in the area by Red & White.

The anomaly of Caledonian Omnibus Co, the only Tilling company in Scotland, was solved by transferring it in January 1950 to the BTC-controlled Western SMT company.

With BTC as the single shareholder for all of the Tilling Group, two holding companies with historic names were quickly placed in voluntary liquidation — Tilling Motor Services and National Omnibus & Transport Co. The Tilling name as an operator survived when the London-based private hire business resurfaced as Thomas Tilling (BTC) Ltd.

The 1947 Electricity Act brought the Midland General group of companies (Midland General, Mansfield District and Notts & Derby) into national ownership, and these were soon under BTC control.

Under BTC ownership the Tilling Group company boards were streamlined, and these reported to a small Management Board. Much local autonomy was given to individual director/general managers, and traffic managers, chief engineers and company secretaries of the operating companies met at regular intervals to discuss common problems and future developments.

The Tilling Association Ltd, formed before BTC days, continued to act as a central organisation for the group, arranging insurance, central purchasing, publicity and bulk-buying contracts. BET had an equivalent organisation, the British Electrical Federation.

It quickly became clear after BTC had grown in its early years, and achieved its peak passenger carryings and fleet size in the mid-1950s, that the bus industry was facing a steady decline in passenger numbers as Britain shook off the years of austerity and headed to a prosperity that allowed more families to own a motorcar and a television set, changing travelling habits for all time.

The 1962 Transport Act rang down the curtain on BTC and brought a new set of initials, THC (Transport Holding Company), and a new structure for the nationalised transport industry. Two significant parts of BTC were hived off separately as the British Railways Board (BRB) and the London Transport Board, so THC inherited the rest of the old BTC bus interests, except for the former railway company interests in bus services jointly with the municipalities of Halifax, Huddersfield, Sheffield and Todmorden, which rather surprisingly passed to BRB. Otherwise the railways now had no financial links with the nationalised bus companies.

Looking back on 15 years of BTC, the Tilling Group companies represented important investments for the commission, over a period when British Railways was consistently losing a substantial amount of money. The annual

▼ Many of the Tilling Group companies had a requirement for dual-purpose single-deckers that were equally at home on bus duties, or as private hire or relief express coaches. Wilts & Dorset No 521 (JAM 225), a 1953 Bristol LS6G with ECW 'express' body, complete with 41 high-back seats, and painted in an attractively non-standard red/black/cream livery, on a private hire at the Tower of London when new. *F. G. Reynolds*

Later in life, Tilling Group companies often sought to rebuild single-deck coaches for further work as buses or dual-purpose vehicles. Cumberland No 275 (NRM 372), a 1954 Bristol LS6G with ECW coach body, had received a new destination box, a folding door, and bus-type seats for further service when photographed in June 1967. *R. L. Wilson*

Durham District Services was formed by BTC to marry three important Co Durham independents operating in what was largely Northern General territory. No DL1 (177 AHN), a 1956 Bristol LD6B with 60-seat ECW body, is seen at Darlington. *Arnold Richardson/Photobus*

The trend-setting Bristol RE chassis offered Tilling companies single-deck buses with seats for 54, just one fewer than lowbridge Bristol K types. West Yorkshire No SRG11 (GWU 810C), a 1965 RELL6G with ECW body, at Harrogate bus station. *G. W. Dickson*

Lincolnshire No 2328 (NBE 131), a 1956 Bristol Lodekka LD6B with 60-seat ECW body. *Arnold Richardson/Photobus*

The Tilling Group believed in investing in infrastructure, constructing new bus stations, garages and workshops for many of its companies. This general view of Lincoln's new bus station, shown just after it opened in March 1959, shows the enclosed platforms, with the inspector's office on the right. Lincolnshire vehicles visible include, on the extreme left, a Bristol SC4LK with the coach version of the ECW body, and, in the centre, a Bristol MW in green/white express livery. *Ian Allan library*

reports published by BTC seem rather more concerned with the problems faced by the railways than they were in the profitable operations of the bus companies, which seem to have been allowed to beaver away without exciting much comment from the commission. This was doubtless the way the Tilling Group wanted it.

The THC era was to prove to be a brief one. Always susceptible to political whims and changes in government, the transport industry had faced increasing problems in the 1950s and 1960s. The passenger decline was just one of the problems — others were the need to cut or withdraw unremunerative services, the regular rises in fares levels, a chronic shortage of platform staff in some areas, and the increasing industrial unrest that resulted in strikes and other industrial action following disagreements with management over pay rates and conditions, and shift-working patterns.

Yet another Transport Act spelt out the end of THC and the Tilling Group, and resulted in some of the most far-reaching

changes in the industry since 1948. The Labour government decided to place London Transport under the control of the Greater London Council, to create Passenger Transport Executives (PTEs) in four major conurbations in England, to set up the Scottish Transport Group to control Scottish Bus Group and ferry companies, and to create the National Bus Company (NBC) to bring together the state-owned bus companies in England and Wales. With the threat of compulsory acquisition once again hanging over the heads of bus operators, the BET Group decided that it no longer wished to be involved in bus operation in the UK and sold the balance of its bus interests to THC late in 1967 for £35 million.

At one time it looked as if Tilling and BET would continue to act as separate units within THC, but when the details of the 1968 Transport Act were made known, it was clear that the opportunity had been taken to weld the two very different groups into one new all-embracing NBC.

► Crosville's new Crewe bus station and garage in June 1960. This was a more typical style of station, with open loading bays and a covered passenger accommodation. Parked at the stands in preparation for the opening are three Bristol MW coaches. The information bus on the left was a converted Beadle/Leyland Cub rebuild. *Ian Allan library*

▲ Tilling companies boasted substantial central workshops with staff who could turn their hand to a variety of engineering, coachbuilding, painting, trimming and machining skills to keep the fleet on the road. This 1957 view inside the body shop at Eastern National's Chelmsford works shows, from the left, a 1956 Bristol LD5G Lodekka, a 1939 Bristol K5G with ECW 48-seat lowbridge body, a Bedford OWB/Duple, a Bristol L5G/ECW, a Bristol L6B/ECW coach and a Leyland Tiger PS1/Duple. It is interesting that the 18-year-old K5G is receiving body attention. *Ian Allan library*

◄ Standard Bristol/ECW buses started to dominate the Tilling fleets at an early stage. Wilts & Dorset No 269 (EAM 612), an immaculate 1947 K6A (with AEC 7.7-litre engine) with 55-seat lowbridge body, is seen at Salisbury early in its life in the company of prewar examples. *F. G. Reynolds*

Better Flavour! **Ty·Phoo Tea** Money Saver!

ALFRETON

WESTHOUSES
TIBSHELF
TEMPLE NORMANTON

08

Mansfield District buses sported this unique interpretation of the green/cream livery, as worn here in May 1963 by No 526 (562 ERR), a 1960 Bristol Lodekka FS6G with 60-seat ECW body. *R. L. Wilson*

The associated Midland General and Notts & Derby companies wore an attractive blue/cream livery, here on Midland General No 478 (516 JRA), a 1959 Bristol LD6G with 58-seat ECW body, in Chesterfield bus station in October 1962. *G. W. Dickson*

United Counties No 145 (WBD 145), a 1961 Bristol MW6G with ECW 45-seat body, passes garden city homes typical of Letchworth on its way to Hitchin.
S. J. Butler collection

Exhibitions of new vehicles were a popular way to attract the public to coach travel in the 1950s. Inside the London Coastal Coaches garage at Eccleston Place, London in April 1954 are three Bristol LS types with ECW 39-seat coach bodies, all subtly different for what is remembered as a highly-standardised design. From left to right they are United Auto No BUT5 (SHN 720), a 1953 LS6B in Tyne-Tees-Thames khaki/cream, with illuminated United name above the destination screens; South Midland No 95 (TWL 60), a fairly standard 1953 LS6B; and Royal Blue (Southern National) No 1298 (OTT 98), a 1953 LS6G, with distinctive destination display.
Ian Allan library

The famous Hants & Dorset bus and coach station at the Square, Bournemouth, with the open-air bus station on the upper level and the coach station on the lower level. This 1959 view shows an interesting selection of buses, including the inevitable Bristol K, L and LD variants, and oddities like Northern Counties-bodied AEC Regent IIIs and, in the foreground, what appears to be a Dutfield-bodied Bristol L6B.
Ian Allan library

▲

Even after the Lodekka became available, some Tilling fleets continued to favour the Bristol K type with the more spacious ECW highbridge body style. Brighton, Hove & District bought no Lodekkas until 1959, and its last Ks were, unusually, KS6G types, where the 8ft-wide KSW had normally been favoured, and were for use on routes serving narrow streets. No 493 (MPM 493), seen when new in 1957, was one of this final batch of KS6Gs, which were among the last K types built. The highbridge ECW body has seats for 62, unusually high on a K. *H. Frier*

▲

Although much Tilling territory was rural, and Crosville had its fair share of rural routes, lanes as narrow as this were relatively uncommon. No SMG374 (350 MFM), a 1959 Bristol MW6G with 41-seat ECW bus body, squeezes down the lanes to Melin-y-Coed, near Llanrwst, on a market day service. *A. Moyes*

United Counties No 107
(MNV 766), a 1956 Bristol
LS5G with 41-seat ECW bus
body, seen in July 1969.
R. L. Wilson

A more ambitious conversion of a Bristol/ECW LS coach. Crosville No EUG319 (OFM 691), a 1953 LS6G with a new ECW bus-style front end, which sits quite happily on the older coach body. It is at New Brighton in July 1965. *R. L. Wilson*

In June 1967, Eastern Counties No LM991 (491 DPW), a Bristol MW5G with ECW 45-seat bus body. *R. L. Wilson*

Cumberland's fleet of Leylands, including buses taken into the fleet after nationalisation, lingered on for many years. No 335 (LRM 109), one of 10 lowbridge Leyland-bodied Titan PD2/12 buses delivered in 1952, reverses out of the Whitehaven garage. These were to be Cumberland's last Leylands under Tilling control. *Michael Dryhurst*

3. The Tilling Companies

Commenting in *Bus & Coach* magazine in November 1942 about the recently completed reorganisation of the bus industry that resulted in the creation of separate Tilling and BET groupings of bus companies, L. D. Kitchin wrote: 'Generalisations on the effects of this allocation [of territory] are apt to be hazardous, but it does seem that on balance the Tilling areas will still be predominantly those in which one has to work the hardest in order to make a profit.' The division of companies, which seems odd now looking back nearly 50 years, obviously seemed strange to contemporary commentators. Kitchin also wrote: 'Broadly speaking, the companies controlled hitherto by Thomas Tilling operate under conditions which mean that they have to work very hard for their revenue, much of their territory being relatively sparsely populated, as in the case of the three National companies, for example, so that those companies' profits have been made out of strict economy in expenditure, so to speak, rather than out of an abundant revenue. The BET companies, on the other hand, have on the whole enjoyed rather more favourable conditions, as typified by the positions of the Midland Red and Northern General, whose areas include a high proportion of industrial activity, especially in the case of the former.'

Tilling's reasons for taking Crosville, Cumberland and Lincolnshire in exchange for East Midland and North Western, companies that had previously been in the Tilling camp, may never be known, but the 1942 agreement set the ownership pattern for the next 26 years.

The THC set up 'coherent and regional groupings' of its bus companies, and it seemed that these would provide an element of mutual support between the stronger and weaker companies, and these often linked the operators with little chance of expansion, with those who found themselves in more profitable areas.

Using the 1963 groupings, we shall look at the individual Tilling Group companies, their background, their operating area and their fleet policy. In the vehicle information, the Bristol style was to suffix the type designation with engine details. So the Gardner 5LW engine (or its horizontal equivalent, the 5HLW) was designated 5G, the Gardner 6LW or 6LX (or their 6HLW or 6HLX horizontal equivalents) were 6G; the Bristol AVW (or from 1958 BVW) and horizontal LSW engines were 6B. These were the main variants, but 6A was used for the AEC 7.7-litre engine, and 6L for the Leyland O.600. In the smaller Bristol chassis, the 4LK designation signified the Gardner 4LK engine, and the suffix 4A the horizontal four-cylinder Albion EN250 engine.

Starting in the north, the Northern group comprised Cumberland, Durham District, United Auto and West Yorkshire. In 1963 these companies contributed 11.45% of the Tilling Group's gross revenue.

Cumberland Motor Services Ltd

Cumberland Motor Services Ltd was formed in 1921 when BAT acquired a 50% shareholding in the Whitehaven Motor Service Co Ltd. It became a T&BAT subsidiary in 1928, and from 1929 the LMS railway and Tilling Motor Services held just under one-third share each. The balance was held by the Meageen family, which had started the Whitehaven company and which retained its shareholding until nationalisation. The Cumberland name was an ambitious one when it was coined in 1921, but gradually the company spread to become a territorial company based in Whitehaven and reaching northeast to Carlisle, with important trunk services between the two, and between Whitehaven and Keswick, with infrequent services to the other towns and villages in the area.

The Cumberland fleet was Leyland dominated well into BTC days, as forward orders placed by the Meageens tied the company into Leylands until 1952, although some did appear with ECW bodies. Cumberland's first 'standard' Bristol/ECW purchases were in 1954, and from that time it took LS and LD models, followed by SC, MW, FS, FSF, FLF and RELL types. Cumberland territory doubtless dictated the use of more powerful engines than the Gardner 5LW, and so most deliveries had six-cylinder Gardner engines, with some Bristol engines as well. A reminder of the previous regime was the choice of Leyland engines for its 1964 FLF Lodekkas and later RELLs, and Leyland 400 engines were fitted in Bedford VAL14s with Duple coach bodies bought in 1965.

Durham District Services Ltd

Durham District Services Ltd (DDS), as already described, was formed in 1950 to operate services taken over from ABC Motors, Darlington Triumph and Express Omnibus. These independents operated in County Durham, in an area stretching between Sunderland in the north, Darlington in the south, Barnard Castle to the west, and Middlesbrough in the east. This was well inside the territory of the BET-owned Northern General group companies, and if these services had been placed under the control of Tilling's United Auto company, a pooling agreement would have come into force, so

the new subsidiary, under United control, was created.

Durham District started with a ragbag of buses inherited from the acquired companies, but soon United started drafting in older Bristols from its own fleet, and gradually the DDS fleet was updated with Bristol/ECW LS, MW, LD, FSF and FLF buses. DDS was absorbed by United in July 1968.

United Automobile Services Ltd

United Automobile Services Ltd was, for some years, one of the most important operators to remain independent of the Tilling and BET empires. Founded in Lowestoft in 1912 by E. B. Hutchinson, the company expanded not only throughout Norfolk and into Lincolnshire, but into County Durham. By 1928 it was operating over 600 buses, and was clearly a prize for the new bus groupings or for the railways which had gained road transport powers around this time. United became almost a pawn in the battles between T&BAT and the main-line railway companies, and its eventual purchase, jointly by T&BAT and LNER in 1929, paved the way for other joint purchases which gave the railway companies an involvement in bus operation without the bus groupings abdicating control.

The new owners decided to split what had grown into an extensive company, and the East Anglian interests became part of the new Eastern Counties company. United was now centred in the northeast of England, covering an area that stretched from North Yorkshire in the south right to Berwick-upon-Tweed. This was not continuous territory, for BET's Northern General group occupied a small but intensely urban and profitable area in Tyneside, Wearside and County Durham.

United was an important express service operator, with its daytime and overnight Newcastle/Middlesbrough/Darlington-London (Tyne-Tees-Thames) services, as well as seasonal services to east and west coast holiday resorts. Many of its bus services were lengthy trunk runs, like Newcastle-Carlisle, Darlington-West Hartlepool, Durham-Middlesbrough, Bishop Auckland-Sunderland and Ripon-York. There were also services to Edinburgh and Glasgow jointly with Scottish Omnibuses. United operated town services in Carlisle and Scarborough.

Eastern National operated an extensive holiday tour programme, and Bristol MW6G coach, No 356 (10 DLY), with the original version of the revised MW coach body from ECW, with stepped waistrail, waits on a Scottish pier in August 1964. The 34-seat coach had been new in 1962 to Tilling, and passed to Eastern National in 1963. *R. L. Wilson*

Brighton Hove & District worked closely with Brighton Corporation and BH&D buses wore the Corporation's attractive red/cream livery. No 2063 (DAP 63C), a 1965 Bristol FS6G with 60-seat ECW body, complete with cream window rubbers, sits at Old Steine in Brighton in June 1971 (after BH&D had been merged into the Southdown fleet), with a Corporation Leyland PD2/Weymann on the right. *Dave Brown*

In the York-West Yorkshire
fleet, jointly owned with the
city authorities, No YDG90
(OWT 203), a prewar Bristol
K5G, rebuilt and rebodied
with a highbridge 56-seat
ECW body, and re-
registered, passes under the
city walls in York.
Arnold Richardson/Photobus

United Auto was a committed Bristol/ECW customer from the 1930s, and operated most types. Its highly-standardised single-deck fleet moved from L and LL models to LS and MW types in the 1950s. United operated the prototype RELL bus, and went on to build up a substantial fleet. There were also RELH coaches, and examples of the shorter RESL bus. United also bought the small SUL4A bus, for more deeply rural duties, and from 1968 built up a substantial fleet of LHs.

Double-deckers ranged from K and KSW types, mostly lowbridge but with highbridge examples for town services. Lodekka variants were the LD, FS, FSF and FLF types.

West Yorkshire Road Car Co Ltd

West Yorkshire Road Car Co Ltd was formed in 1927 from the Harrogate Road Car Co. The Harrogate company had passed to T&BAT in 1924, renamed Harrogate & District, and in 1929 the LMS and LNE railways each bought roughly one-quarter share, with Tilling holding roughly half.

In Keighley and York, West Yorkshire entered agreements with the local corporations to run buses in place of municipal buses and trams. Keighley-West Yorkshire Services, jointly owned by West Yorkshire and Keighley Corporation, was set up in 1932 to replace trolleybuses and motorbuses. York-West Yorkshire Joint Committee was set up in 1934.

West Yorkshire bought the substantial Armley, Leeds-based Samuel Ledgard business in 1967.

The West Yorkshire route network was centred, geographically, on Harrogate, with routes in the south, around Leeds and Bradford, north to Ripon and Thirsk, west to Skipton and Colne, and east to York and Malton. Frequent trunk services included Leeds-Bradford, Harrogate-Ripon, Leeds-York and Bradford-Ilkley. Its main express services were the seasonal Leeds-Skipton-

◄ West Yorkshire's sole Bristol Lodekka FSF6B with 60-seat forward entrance ECW body, No DX82 (YWW 77), in Otley Road, Leeds in June 1963. *R. F. Mack*

Keswick/Morecambe routes, joint with Ribble, and the Keighley-Scarborough service. It was also involved in the Yorkshire Services pool with BET's East Midland, East Yorkshire, Northern General, Yorkshire Traction and Yorkshire Woollen companies. These operated express services between Yorkshire and London, and Yorkshire and the West Midlands.

Like United, West Yorkshire had been an avid Bristol/ECW customer long before the Tilling & BAT split-up. In the postwar period it too had examples of most vehicle types. The Bristol L was popular, in L, LL and LWL forms as buses and coaches, followed by the LS, MW and RELL/RELH. Lowbridge and highbridge K types were bought, in K, KS and KSW forms, before moving on to the Lodekka (West Yorkshire owned the second prototype) in LD, FS and FSF forms. Other single-deck types were SUL4A buses, RELL buses and RELH coaches.

The next Tilling grouping was called East Midland, covering the Lincolnshire, Mansfield District, Midland General, Notts & Derby and United Counties companies. This was a more unusual grouping, encompassing companies from widely varying backgrounds. In 1963 these companies contributed 13.85% of the Tilling Group's gross revenue.

Lincolnshire Road Car Co Ltd

Lincolnshire Road Car Co Ltd was formed in 1928 under T&BAT control from Silver Queen's operations in the area, and in 1929 the LNE and LMS railways invested capital equal to the Tilling holding. From that time it grew by acquisition of a large number of local independents.

Its operating area stretched down the east coast from the Humber to The Wash, with Lincoln as its centre, and reaching as far afield as Doncaster, Nottingham and Leicester. The main bus services included routes from Lincoln to Grantham, Sleaford and Newark, Grantham to Leicester and Nottingham, Boston-Spalding, and Spalding-King's Lynn. Express services were Cleethorpes-Skegness-Lincoln-Peterborough-London, and seasonal services linking with holiday resorts on the east coast.

Lincolnshire had been a keen Leyland customer until nationalisation in 1948, and from then it received a range of Bristol/ECW types. There were L, LL and LWL buses and coaches; LS and MW buses and coaches; SC4LK rural buses; RELL buses and RELH coaches; and LHs from 1968. The double-deck fleet included lowbridge Leyland PD1As bought in 1948, then the highbridge Bristol K, KS and KSW. These were followed by Lodekkas of LD, FS and FL types. Non-standard coaches were Duple-bodied Bedford VAM70s bought in 1968.

Mansfield District Traction Co

Mansfield District Traction Co was one of the more unusual Tilling Group companies. Its roots were in the Mansfield & District Light Railway Co, operating trams from 1905. The following year Mansfield District Tramways Ltd was formed and this subsequently became Mansfield District Omnibus Co Ltd, and Mansfield District Traction Co in 1929. Ownership passed to the Balfour Beatty group's Midland Counties Electric Supply Co Ltd. Tram services stopped in 1932 and though trolleybuses were considered, motorbuses took over. The company grew through acquisition and in 1947 the shareholding of the Midland Counties company was vested in the new British Electricity Authority. The bus services passed to BTC in 1948.

The last trolleybuses operated by a Tilling company were owned by Brighton, Hove & District, running jointly with Brighton Corporation until 1960. BH&D No 343 (CPM 375), a 1939 AEC 661T with Weymann 56-seat body, is seen turning into Old Steine, Brighton, in March 1959. Although new in 1939, these buses did not enter service until 1946. *Michael Dryhurst*

Throughout England and Wales there were towns where the territorial companies met. In many cases Tilling Group companies met up with BET companies, but at Salisbury the visiting green Hants & Dorset buses met the local red Wilts & Dorset ones. H&D No 1506 (BEL 679B) prepares to return to Bournemouth, while in the background W&D No 570 (LWV 846), a 1955 Bristol LS5G/ECW 41-seat bus is parked, and No 393 (KHR 530), a 1954 Bristol KSW6B/ECW lowbridge 55-seater, sets off for Andover. *R. G. Funnell*

▲ As with the other Balfour Beatty fleets, Mansfield District favoured AECs, and operated many Regals and Regents, as well as Guy Arabs bought during the war.

The first Tilling-style vehicles were Bristol/ECW LS and LD deliveries in 1954, and later MW, FS, FSF and FLF types were bought. Bedford VAM70 coaches with Duple bodywork were bought in 1968.

Midland General Omnibus Co Ltd/ Nottinghamshire & Derbyshire Traction Co

Midland General Omnibus Co Ltd (MGOC) was set up by the Nottingham & Derbyshire Tramways Company in 1920 to operate feeder buses to the Notts & Derby tram routes. The trams were replaced by trolleybuses in 1933, and the company was renamed the Nottinghamshire & Derbyshire Traction Co (N&D). Midland General grew as a bus operator in the 1920s and 1930s by acquiring several local operators and assumed responsibility for the Notts & Derby company following withdrawal of the N&D trolleybuses, although the Notts & Derby fleetname continued. With Mansfield District, Midland General and Notts & Derby passed to the British Electricity Authority, and then to the BTC in 1948.

Midland General and Notts & Derby operated in a compact but well-populated area between Nottingham in the south and Chesterfield in the north, serving such towns as Matlock, Alfreton, Ripley, Heanor, Ilkeston, Hucknall and Sutton-in-Ashfield. Seasonal express services were operated to seaside resorts on the east and west coasts of England from various towns in the two companies' operating areas.

Like Mansfield District, the MGOC and N&D fleets were dominated by AECs for the first years in state control, but standard Bristol/ECW products started to arrive in 1953. The three Balfour Beatty companies usually managed to standardise on six-cylinder Gardner engines, and MGOC and N&D took KSW, LS, MW, LD, FS, FSF, FLF (including the last Lodekka built) and RESH and RELH models. The Midland General and Notts & Derby fleets were operated as a single unit, in a blue/cream livery that was unique in the Tilling Group.

United Counties Omnibus Co Ltd

United Counties Omnibus Co Ltd started life as the Wellingborough Motor Omnibus Co in 1913 and adopted the title United Counties in 1921 (The United Counties Omnibus & Road Transport Co Ltd), though this was simplified in 1933. Thomas Tilling Ltd bought the company in 1931, but there was no railway interest. In 1952 Eastern National's Midland area was transferred to United Counties, along with 240 buses.

The United Counties territory, centred on Northampton, stretched north to Stamford, Peterborough and Oakham, west to Daventry and Towcester, south to Oxford, Amersham, Luton and Hitchin, and east to Royston, Cambridge and

◄ The blue/cream-painted Midland General fleet started to receive standard-issue Bristol/ECW vehicles from 1954. No 234 (XNU 415), a 1955 LS6G with dual-purpose 43-seat body, is seen on private hire work in Moreton-in-the-Marsh, in the Cotswolds, in September 1956. *Ian Allan library*

St Ives. Its geographical position meant that it connected with a number of other territorial operators — City of Oxford, Eastern Counties, Lincolnshire, London Transport, Midland Red and Thames Valley.

United Counties, as a Tilling company from the 1930s, was a good Bristol/ECW customer. In BTC days it bought L, LL and LWL, LS and MW types in bus, dual-purpose and coach forms, SC4LK and SUS4A types for more lightly-loaded work, and RELL buses and RELH coaches. Lowbridge K and KSW types were followed by LD, FS and FLF type Lodekkas.

Crosville Motor Services Ltd

The only company in Tilling's northwestern area was Crosville Motor Services Ltd, one of the largest in the group, contributing 11.55% of the Tilling Group's gross revenue in 1963.

The unusual Crosville name reflects the names of George Crosland-Taylor and Georges Ville, who went into partnership to build Crosville cars, but few were sold and Crosville became a bus operator in 1911, working between Chester and Ellesmere Port, and soon to Crewe, Nantwich and Sandbach. Further expansion took the company into other parts of Cheshire and into Liverpool.

In 1929 the LMS railway bought Crosville to gain experience in the bus business, renaming it LMS (Crosville). The purchase led to further expansion into North Wales, and from 1930 T&BAT held a shareholding equal to that of the railway holding. Further railway interest in Crosville came with the merger with Western Transport Co Ltd in 1933; this was a T&BAT company with GWR involvement.

Crosville covered a substantial area, with services ranging from high-frequency urban routes in Cheshire and Liverpool, to deeply rural services in North Wales. Frequent services

Tilling's Isle of Wight operator was Southern Vectis, whose No 548 (ODL 8), a 1957 Bristol LD6G/ECW 60-seater, is seen in June 1966 heading for Freshwater. *R. L. Wilson*

The coaches of Thames Valley's South Midland fleet were painted in a distinctive maroon/cream, as on No 90 (TWL 55), a 1953 Bristol LS6B with 37-seat ECW coach body, seen in September 1959. Note the awkward outward-opening door. *R. L. Wilson*

▲ included Chester-Birkenhead, Chester-Rhyl, Birkenhead-Loggerheads, Chester-Runcorn, Birkenhead-Heswall, Liverpool-Warrington, Chester-Llangollen, Llandudno-Caernarvon, Rhyl-Llandudno, Bangor-Holyhead, and Blaenau Ffestiniog-Pwllheli. Crosville operated express services from Liverpool/Chester to London, from various points to Welsh resorts, and from its own area to Blackpool.

The company had been a staunch Leyland fan, but soon built up a typically Tilling Bristol/ECW fleet, with L, LL and LWL types, LS and MW types, RESL and RELL buses, RELH coaches, and SC4LK buses and coaches. The double-deck fleet ▼ included lowbridge K and KSW models, followed by LD, FS, FSF and FLF Lodekkas. Most engine options were taken, including the AEC 7.7-litre unit in early postwar K types. Bedford VAM5 coaches with Duple bodywork were bought in 1967.

Tilling's Eastern area comprised Eastern Counties, Eastern National and Tillings Transport. In 1963 these companies contributed 14.45% of the Tilling Group's gross revenue.

Tilling Group buses often carried house advertising, like this United Counties Lodekka in Luton, promoting the express coach services from Nottingham/Leicester/Northampton to London. No 701 (GRP 701D) is an FS6B model of 1966, with 60-seat ECW bodywork. *S. J. Butler collection*

Eastern Counties used highbridge double-deckers on town services, like No LKH93 (HPW 93), a 1948 Bristol K5G with 56-seat ECW body, passing Peterborough Town Hall in 1956. *Ian Allan library*

Eastern Counties Omnibus Co Ltd

Eastern Counties Omnibus Co Ltd (ECOC) was set up in 1931 to combine four T&BAT operators – Eastern Counties Road Car, Ortona, Peterborough Electric Traction, and United Auto's East Anglian area. United retained a share of the new company, and there were LMS and LNE railway shareholdings. The new Eastern Counties company also inherited the United coachworks at Lowestoft, which from 1936 traded as Eastern Coach Works.

ECOC took over the Norwich Electric Tramways Co in 1933, which gave it Norwich town services.

Based in Norwich, ECOC covered Norfolk and parts of Suffolk, across to Cambridge and Peterborough and south to Ipswich. Principal services included routes from Norwich to Cromer and Great Yarmouth, from King's Lynn to Hunstanton and Wisbech, Royston-Cambridge, and Ipswich to Felixstowe and Colchester.

A number of express services were operated, including Great Yarmouth-Bury St Edmunds-London, Cromer-Norwich-Cambridge-London, and other less frequent services linking London with other towns in the ECOC area.

Although ECOC built up a typical Tilling Group fleet of Bristol/ECW models — L, LL, LWL, LS, MW, SC, RELH, RELL and RELH single-deckers, K, KS, KSW, LD, FS, FL and FLF double-deckers — there were also non-standard types, some as a result of acquisitions. So there were examples of Albion, Dennis, Foden and Maudslay chassis in the fleet, as well as semi-chassisless Bedford-Beadles and ECW-bodied Dennises. There were also 18 Duple-bodied Bedford coaches bought in 1954. The ECW connection meant that ECOC operated prototypes — one of the first LSs and the first SC. In a predominantly flat area the use of Gardner five-cylinder engines was widespread, and some Bristol L types and the LS prototype even had four-cylinder Gardners.

Eastern National Omnibus Co

Eastern National Omnibus Co (ENOC) traces its ancestry back to the Chelmsford operations of the National Steam Car Co, later National Omnibus & Transport. Following investment by the LMS and LNER companies, Eastern National was formed in 1930. After nationalisation ENOC's area was more clearly defined when its Midland area was transferred to United Counties. BTC acquired the business of Hicks of Braintree in 1950, and placed it in ENOC control. Two years later Tilling's Westcliff-on-Sea company was placed in ENOC control. In 1963 ENOC took over the business of Moore's of Kelvedon.

The Eastern National area covered Essex and parts of Suffolk. Principal services included Chelmsford-Southend, Bishops Stortford-Saffron Walden, Clacton-Southend, Tilbury-Clacton, Southend-Grays, and Colchester-Walton-on-the-Naze.

Express services linked Halstead, Braintree, Clacton and Chelmsford with London.

The fleet included Bristol/ECW single-deckers of L, LL, LWL, LS, MW, SC and RELH types, and K, KS, KSW, LD, LDL, FS and FLF type double-deckers. Oddments included Beadle-Bedford semi-chassisless buses in the early postwar period, and Bedford SB13/Duple Firefly coaches in 1964, as well as buses acquired from other operators.

Tilling's Southern area included the Brighton, Hove & District, Hants & Dorset, Newbury & District, South Midland, Southern Vectis, Thames Valley, Venture and Wilts & Dorset companies. In 1963 they contributed 15.69% of the group's gross revenue.

Brighton, Hove & District Omnibus Co Ltd

Brighton, Hove & District Omnibus Co Ltd (BH&D) was formed in 1935 to take over Thomas Tilling's Brighton area services, which had first started in 1916. This had been the first major Tilling excursion outside London, and from 1939 BH&D entered an agreement with Brighton Corporation to run co-ordinated services. This agreement caused BH&D to run trolleybuses for 20 years, and meant that its buses were painted in Brighton's red/cream livery, rather than Tilling red/cream. In 1961 the agreement was further amended to include the

▲ Looking out of place in Eastern National livery, No 2004 (GYL 983) was a wartime Guy Arab II with postwar Strachans body, acquired with the business of Moore Bros of Kelvedon in 1963. The bus had originated with Birch Bros. It is seen at Tolleshunt Knights in 1965. *G. R. Mills*

Bristol Omnibus Co coaches carried the historic Bristol Greyhound name and logo, as worn here by 974 WAE, a Bristol RELH6G with ECW coach bodywork, photographed in 1971. *R. L. Wilson*

Bristol's subsidiary Cheltenham District fleet carried this distinguished maroon/cream livery. This is No 7185 (BHY 716C), a 1965 Bristol FLF6G with 70-seat ECW forward entrance body, seen in May 1970. *R. L. Wilson*

In Thames Valley's South Midland fleet, painted maroon/cream, No C432 (613 JPU), a 1957 Bristol LS6G with 34-seat ECW coach body, turns into Victoria Coach Station in London in August 1958. The coach was acquired from Eastern National.
Ian Allan library

services of its BET Group neighbour, Southdown. BH&D had a compact network of urban services in the Brighton and Hove areas, operated exclusively by double-deckers during the BTC/THC years until a batch of Bristol RESLs was bought. The Tilling-influenced fleet had included many AECs, and when trolleybuses were bought these were AECs and AEC-built BUTs. Bristol/ECW types operated by BH&D were K, KS, KSW, LDS, FS, FSF, FLF and RESL models.

Hants & Dorset Motor Services Ltd

Hants & Dorset Motor Services Ltd (H&D) grew out of Bournemouth & District Motor Services, and following Tilling's purchase of an interest in this company in 1920, it assumed the more familiar Hants & Dorset title. H&D became part of the T&BAT combine, and in 1929 Southern Railway

bought a shareholding. In 1964 H&D and neighbour Wilts & Dorset were placed under common management.

Hants & Dorset's main routes included frequent services from Bournemouth to Lymington, Salisbury and Swanage, and from Southampton to Lymington, Salisbury and Winchester.

The H&D fleet included Bristol/ECW L, LL, LWL, LS, MW, RELL and RELH type single-deckers and K, KSW, LD, LDL, FS, FL and FLF type double-deckers. Unusual purchases in the early postwar years included Beadle-Morris Commercial lightweight single-deckers, and AEC Regent III and Leyland Titan PD2 double-deckers. Beadle and Portsmouth Aviation also built bodies for H&D on Bristol L chassis.

Newbury & District Motor Services Ltd/South Midland Motor Services Ltd/ Venture Ltd

Newbury & District Motor Services Ltd, South Midland Motor Services Ltd and Venture Ltd were Red & White group subsidiaries which had been acquired in the 1940s and following the sale to BTC in 1950 were placed under the control of Tilling fleets. Newbury & District went to Thames Valley, and its services were quickly absorbed. South Midland, primarily a coach operator, also passed to Thames Valley, which used the name on its coach fleet. Venture passed to Wilts & Dorset.

Southern Vectis Omnibus Co Ltd

Southern Vectis Omnibus Co Ltd was the Tilling Group's Isle of Wight company, formed out of the Vectis company created by Dodson Bros in the early 1920s. The Southern Railway bought the Vectis company in 1929, resulting in the change of name, and T&BAT soon acquired a share equal to the railway's.

The Southern Vectis territory was clearly defined by the geography of the Isle of Wight, with principal services between Ryde and Cowes, Newport and Sandown, Ryde and Bembridge, Newport and Freshwater, and Ryde and Ventnor.

Variety was added to the Bristol/ECW fleet of L, LL, LWL, LS, MW, SUL, RESL, LH, K, KS, KSW, LD, FS and FLF types with Duple-bodied Bedford coaches — SB8, SB13, VAL14 and VAM70 models. There were also rare Bristol RESH6G coaches with Duple bodywork.

Thames Valley Traction Co Ltd

Thames Valley Traction Co Ltd grew out of BAT's Reading branch, and came into T&BAT ownership in 1928. The Great Western and Southern railways bought into Thames Valley.

Based in Reading, Thames Valley operated south to Basingstoke and Camberley, west to Swindon and Hungerford, north to Oxford and Aylesbury, and east to Slough, Windsor and Sunningdale.

Its principal bus services included the frequent routes from Reading to Maidenhead, Windsor, Camberley and Newbury, High Wycombe to Windsor and Aylesbury, and Newbury to Oxford.

Express services were operated between Reading and London, one route via Wokingham and Ascot, and the hourly service via Maidenhead.

The Thames Valley fleet included the usual Bristol/ECW mix of L, LL, LWL, LS, MW, SC, RESL, RELL and LH type single-deckers, and K, KSW, LD, LDL and FLF double-deckers. Oddities included Windover-bodied L6B coaches in 1948/50, and Duple-bodied RELH coaches in 1968.

Wilts & Dorset Motor Services Ltd

Wilts & Dorset Motor Services Ltd was started up in 1915 by the men who also set up the Southdown company further along the south coast. It came under the control of T&BAT and the Southern Railway in 1931.

Based in Salisbury, Wilts & Dorset operated regular frequency services from there to Marlborough, Devizes, Trowbridge, Weymouth and Andover, from Andover to Newbury and Basingstoke, and from Basingstoke to Newbury.

Wilts & Dorset had a more varied fleet at nationalisation than others that had already fallen under the Bristol/ECW influence, with AECs, Daimlers and Leylands. Standard

Bristol/ECW types included L, LL, LWL, LS and MW single-deckers, and K, KS, KSW, LD, FS and FLF type double-deckers. Duple-bodied Bedford SB13s were bought in 1965.

The final Tilling area — Western and South Wales — comprised Bath Electric Tramways, Bath Tramways Motor Co, Bristol Omnibus, Cheltenham District, Red & White, Southern National, United Welsh and Western National. In 1963 these companies contributed 15.69% of the Tilling Group's gross revenue.

Bath Electric Tramways Ltd/ Bath Tramways Motor Co Ltd

Bath Electric Tramways Ltd and its subsidiary Bath Tramways Motor Co Ltd passed into the control of the Bristol Tramways company in 1936 though the separate Bath fleetname was maintained. The Bath Tramways company had started a bus service in 1905, and Bristol Tramways took over in 1936.

▲ Thames Valley No 853 (VJB 944), a 1960 Bristol MW6G with 41-seat ECW body, sporting an unusual dual-purpose application of the red/cream livery in May 1969. *R. L. Wilson*

An unusual purchase for Wilts & Dorset in 1967 was a batch of Bedford VAM14s with Willowbrook bodies. No 814 (HWV 326E) is seen in Salisbury bus station in September 1967.
M. Bennett

▲ Bristol Omnibus Co Ltd

Bristol Omnibus Co Ltd was the name adopted in 1957 for the Bristol Tramways & Carriage Co Ltd (BTCC), formed in 1887 from existing tramway, horsebus and cab businesses. BTCC introduced electric trams in 1895 and motorbuses in 1906. Initially the bus services were in the Bristol, Bath, Cheltenham, Gloucester and Weston-super-Mare areas, but soon BTCC had expanded to Stroud and Wells.

BTCC was bought by the GWR in 1929, and the GWR interest in the National Omnibus & Transport Company meant that BTCC found itself in 1931 under Western National control. Thomas Tilling Ltd had bought a controlling interest in NO&T earlier in 1931, so Bristol became an associate company of Tilling.

The extensive BTCC area stretched north to Gloucester and Cheltenham, with routes to Hereford, Great Malvern, Evesham and Broadway; south to Bath and Wells, with routes to Bridgwater, Yeovil, Warminster and Salisbury; east to Swindon and Devizes, with routes to Oxford and Hungerford. A joint committee was formed with Bristol Corporation in

1937, when the corporation exercised its powers to acquire the BTCC tramways in the city.

The Bristol Greyhound name was used on BTCC's coaches, surviving into National Bus Company days. Services were operated between Weston-super-Mare/Bristol and London, and the company was involved in the Associated Motorways network.

Inevitably the fleet was largely Bristol built, and most Bristol/ECW models were operated, including L buses and LWL coaches, LS and MW buses and coaches, SUS buses, and RELH coaches. Double-deckers were K, KS and KSW types in lowbridge and highbridge formats, and LD, LDL, FS, FSF and FLF Lodekkas. The close connection with the Bristol manufacturing arm meant that the bus company operated experimental vehicles, including the LD and LS prototypes.

Cheltenham District Traction Co

Cheltenham District Traction Co, originally a tramway operator, had been part of the Balfour Beatty group before passing to Red & White in 1939, and when Red & White sold out to BTC in 1950 control of Cheltenham District passed to Bristol Tramways. The buses were painted in a dark red/cream livery.

Red & White Services Ltd/ United Welsh Services Ltd

Red & White Services Ltd stemmed from several pioneering bus operators in Gloucestershire and the South Wales valleys which were brought together under the Red & White name from 1929.

United Welsh Services Ltd was set up by Red & White in 1938 to bring together the operations of a number of smaller companies in the Swansea area. The Red & White group functioned without any Tilling or BET involvement, but in 1950 decided to sell out to BTC.

Under Tilling, Red & White territory stretched from Gloucester west to Cardiff and Aberdare and inland to Tredegar, Abergavenny, Monmouth and Hereford. Principal services included Gloucester-Newport, Tredegar-Newport,

The Bath Services name was retained by Bristol Omnibus for its local services in that city. No 1019 (MAE 22F), a 1968 Bristol RELL6L with semi-automatic transmission and ECW 53-seat body, is seen in use on route 14, where these buses were used to replace double-deckers. *P. R. Forsey*

Cheltenham District buses were distinguished by their maroon/cream livery, as worn here in June 1959 by No 85 (OHY 955), a 1951 Bristol KWS6B with 60-seat ECW highbridge body.
R. L. Wilson

Red & White's operations straddled the countryside on both sides of the Wales-England border. Crossing the border at Chepstow Bridge on the Bulwark-Beachley service in June 1965 is No L153 (LAX 624), a 1953 Bristol/ECW Lodekka LD6G with 58-seat rear entrance bodywork, complete with platform doors. This was numerically Red & White's first Bristol, after years of Albion and Guy chassis. The Red & White numbering scheme incorporated the last two figures of the year of delivery.
C. W. Routh

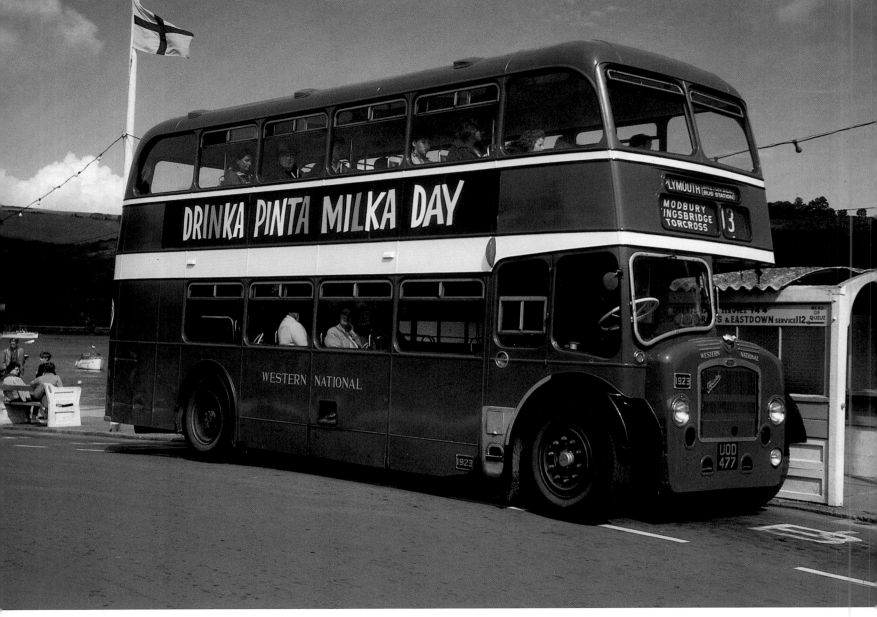

A holiday double-decker as many will remember it from holidays in the West Country, Western National No 1923 (UOD 477), a 1956 Bristol LD6B/ECW 60-seater, at Dartmouth in August 1963.
R. L. Wilson

Sixteen low-cost and attractive 32-seat lightweight ECW chassisless buses were produced in 1950 for Eastern Counties using prewar Dennis Ace parts. No CD844 (HPW 829) displays the once-familiar, but singularly unhelpful, destination RELIEF.
Arnold Richardson/Photobus

Prewar buses still had a role long into the nationalised period, though usually for specialised duties like open-top work in seaside resorts. Southern National No 3821 (FAE 600), a 1938 Bristol K5G with 56-seat ECW body, had been acquired from Bristol Omnibus in 1958.
A. J. Douglas/Photobus

Cardiff-Barry Island, and routes from Newport to Brynmawr and Ebbw Vale. The company was also heavily involved in the Associated Motorways pool.

For many years the Red & White group standardised on Albions, and in the postwar years was buying AEC, Guy and Leyland chassis as well. The first Bristol/ECW products for Red & White were LDs and LSs in 1953, followed by MW, SC, FS, FL, RELL, RELH and RESL models. United Welsh had a similar mix, with the addition of KSW, SUL and FLF types.

Southern National Omnibus Co Ltd/Western National Omnibus Co Ltd

Southern National Omnibus Co Ltd and Western National Omnibus Co Ltd were always closely linked. Formed in 1929 by National Omnibus & Transport and the SR and GWR respectively, they inherited National's West Country operations. In 1931 the National business passed to Tilling. In 1935 the Bournemouth coach operator Elliott Bros, trading as Royal Blue, was acquired jointly with Hants & Dorset, and the Royal Blue name continued on express services.

The companies operated over a substantial part of the West Country, much of it sparsely populated. BET's Devon General company had a chunk of good territory around Exeter and Torbay, leaving the two National companies to serve the rest of Devon and Cornwall, and parts of Somerset and Dorset.

Principal Southern National bus services included Yeovil-Salisbury and Weymouth-Salisbury; Western National services included Plymouth-Torquay and Taunton-Seaton.

The famous Royal Blue express services linked London with Hampshire and the West Country, through a network of frequent services.

Southern/Western National had the usual range of Bristol/ECW types, from L, LL and LWL models through LS, MW, SUL, SUS, RELH, RELL and LH. Lowbridge K, KS and KSW types were operated, followed by LD, LDL, FS and FLF Lodekkas. One of the few VRT/SL6Gs delivered before the formation of National Bus Company went to Western National. Non-standard types in early days were Beadle-bodied Bristol K and L types. Beadle also built some integrals for Western National based on Morris Commercial parts. Unusual purchases in 1967 were Bedford VAM5s with ECW bus bodies.

United Welsh, formerly part of the Red & White group, was also a late convert to standard Tilling-issue buses. No 1244 (JCY 991), a 1953 Bristol/ECW Lodekka LD6G 58-seater, was numerically that fleet's first bus from the Bristol/ECW stables.
Roy Marshall

The lightweight Bristol SU type was ideal for Southern National's operations in the West Country. No 619 (321 EDV), a 1961 Bristol SUL4A with 36-seat ECW body, is seen at West Bay, Bridport, on the town service in October 1971.
R. L. Wilson

Western National No 1970 (469 FTT), a 1960 70-seat Bristol/ECW Lodekka FLF6G, leaves Plymouth's Bretonside bus station, with Royal Blue LS type in the background.
Gordon Turner/Photobus

The Tilling Group was involved in much rebodying of older chassis in the postwar years, often on prewar Bristol chassis that could be brought up to current specification. Midland General, with sturdy Guy chassis which had originally carried utility-style bodies, went to ECW for new bodies. This is No 102 (JNU 680), a 1945 Arab II which received this new 58-seat ECW highbridge body in 1952. It is seen in Langley Mill garage yard in June 1965. *G. W. Dickson*

Non-standard Bristol/ECW L types were supplied to West Yorkshire to permit clearance under this low railway bridge in Leeman Road, York. The low-set destination indicator prevented any problems on York-West Yorkshire No YSG121 (FWX 811), a 1948 L5G with 35-seat body, seen in July 1963. *G. W. Dickson*

ECW's coach body for Bristol L type chassis was surprisingly rounded when compared to the company's bus bodies. The fully-fronted 35-seat body is here fitted to Lincolnshire No 2059 (HBE 513), a 1951 LWL6B, seen in Grantham bus station alongside a Sheffield United Tours AEC Reliance/Plaxton Panorama, in May 1965. *G. W. Dickson*

4. The Tilling Group Fleet

A mixed bag of buses was inherited by the Tilling Group in 1948, and with the Bristol chassis-building works and Eastern Coach Works as BTC subsidiaries, prevented from selling outside the nationalised companies, it seemed likely that the Tilling companies would be quickly stocked with new products from these factories.

There had been a rush to rebuild and rebody older chassis in the early postwar period, and the Tilling companies became involved with a scheme to produce lightweight integral single-deckers from the parts of older buses. Beadle was heavily involved in work of this type, and built buses for Bristol, Eastern National, Hants & Dorset, Lincolnshire, West Yorkshire, Western National and United Auto. These used, variously, Dennis, Leyland and Morris Commercial parts. Later new Bedford OB components were built into Beadle structures for Tilling companies. These useful buses were largely replaced by Bristol's own purpose-built SC type from the mid-1950s.

In 1950 ECW built 16 chassisless single-deck buses for Eastern Counties using parts from that company's prewar Dennis Ace buses. These neat 32-seat buses had Gardner 4LK engines, and an attractive half-cab front end, but no more were built.

Some fleets were already trying to standardise of Bristol and ECW products — often those with a Thomas Tilling, rather than Tilling Motor Services, involvement before the 1942 split-up. Others had a tradition of buying from, for example, AEC or Leyland, and might have been reluctant to trade these relatively refined chassis for the more basic Bristols, which, in fairness, enjoyed a reputation for ruggedness, economy and reliability.

Bristol Tramways had been building buses since 1908, but only in the 1930s did production really take off, partly to suit the requirements of its associated companies in the Tilling Group. The G type double-decker and J type single-decker had been introduced in 1931 with petrol engines, but diesel engines were rapidly being developed at the time and many later chassis had Gardner engines, the start of a long relationship between the chassis and engine builders. A number of G and J types were still in service in 1948, but the most numerous prewar types were their successors, the K and L types.

Introduced in 1937, the K double-decker and L single-decker offered Gardner 5LW engines as standard (K5G and L5G) with the 6LW as an option. The new chassis got off to a good start, but World War 2 interrupted production, and only from 1944 were utility Bristol chassis available, mostly K6A with the AEC A202 7.7-litre engine.

The postwar K and L were announced in 1946, with neater bonnets and radiators, but still with the crash gearboxes when other manufacturers were actively involved in synchromesh or preselective boxes. The K was available in K5G (Gardner 5LW 7.0 litres), K6G (Gardner 6LW 8.4 litres), K6A (AEC A202 7.7 litres) and K6B forms. The K6B had Bristol's new 8.1-litre AVW engine, an engine that was to figure in Bristol chassis until 1958, in both vertical and horizontal (LSW) forms; over 2,800 were built.

The K, for a double-decker 26ft long and 7ft 6in wide, was built from 1946 until a change in regulations led to the 27ft-long KS from 1950, and the 8ft-wide KSW from late 1950. In 1948/9 Bristol had built 20 KW chassis for Cardiff Corporation (26ft x 8ft).

◄ The prototype of the standard postwar Tilling single-decker, United Auto No BLO223 (HHN 223), a 1946 Bristol L5G with 35-seat ECW rear entrance bodywork, photographed near the Lowestoft coachworks — hence the Eastern Counties destination blinds. The square-edged sliding vents were soon replaced by rounded-edge vents within the window rubber. *Ian Allan library*

▲ The ultimate development of the Bristol L was the 30ft-long, 8ft-wide LWL. Western National No 1626 (LTA 785), a 1951 LWL6B with 39-seat ECW body, is seen at Minehead. *M. J. Tozer*

The Bristol K with lowbridge ECW body was the staple double-decker for most Tilling Group companies. United Auto No BGL51 (KHN 494), a 1949 K5G 55-seater, is seen at Redcar in June 1964.
G. W. Dickson

The ultimate version of the long-running Bristol/ECW K type was the longer, wider KSW model. Western National No 1821 (LTA 840) is a 1951 KSW6B with 55-seat ECW lowbridge body.
Arnold Richardson/Photobus

The single-deck L type was developed along similar lines.
The basic L was 27ft 6in long and 7ft 6in wide, the LL was
30ft long, and the LWL was additionally 8ft wide. The same
engine choices were available on the L as on the K, but the
Gardner 5LW and Bristol AVW were the most popular among
Tilling Group companies, with the Bristol engine particularly
favoured in chassis intended for coaching duties.

From 1948/9 flexible engine mounting was introduced on K
and L chassis, vastly improving the vibration and noise levels
that were transmitted from the older solidly-mounted engines.

During the war years ECW had been developing what
became its standard postwar body styles. Production had
moved from Lowestoft to Irthlingborough in
Northamptonshire in 1940, but fewer than 100 new bodies
were built there before production resumed at Lowestoft in
1945/6. Prototype lowbridge and highbridge double-deck
bodies had been completed in 1943/4, and the production
versions were very similar. The lower deck of the lowbridge
and highbridge buses looked broadly similar, but the
lowbridge buses had narrower panelling between the decks,
and a flat, shallow roof; the highbridge buses had more
generously rounded roofs. The style of window that came to

be recognisable on ECW bodies for more than 35 years first
appeared on these buses, and a definite ECW look had been
created.

The single-deck body for Bristol L type chassis had some of
the same characteristics — the rubber-mounted inset windows,
the stylish windscreen — and had an undoubted air of very
satisfying neatness about it. Some of the earliest postwar
bodies had separate square-mounted sliding ventilators above
the side windows, which jarred with the rounded look of
everything else, but soon a style was evolved with a rounded-
top ventilator set within the window rubbers. The single-
deckers had deep cove panelling above the windows, and on
the Tilling standard bodies there was higher-mounted beading
which was designed to allow a greater amount of the relief
colour, as well as allowing space for advertisements. Both the
single-deck and double-deck designs had two-piece destination
displays at the front, with space for the ultimate destination in
the narrower upper box, and space for intermediate points
below. The destination display was repeated at the rear, and
above the entrance on double-deckers; single-deckers had a
single-line display above the side window ahead of the rear
door.

The specification of a rear door on the single-deckers was interesting because many operators were moving to doors behind the front axle, but a neat one-piece sliding door behind the rear axle was the Tilling standard. In later life several Tilling companies converted the bodies on some of their L type chassis to front entrance, to allow for driver-only operation.

Tilling's obsession with standardisation was already clear with these first postwar designs, and although, as so often happens with rigid standardisation, individual requirements would later appear on ECW bodies, the basic bus bodies changed little. Even the moquette chosen was a blend of red and green, suiting the majority of Tilling liveries.

Two shades, Tilling red and Tilling green, were worn by the majority of the group's buses, relieved by cream. The red fleets were Cumberland, Eastern Counties, Red & White, Thames Valley, United Auto, United Welsh and West Yorkshire. The green fleets were Bristol, Crosville, Durham District, Eastern National, Hants & Dorset, Lincolnshire, Southern National, Southern Vectis, United Counties and Western National. The odd fleets were Brighton, Hove & District (Brighton Corporation red/cream), Cheltenham

District (maroon/cream), Mansfield District (green/cream applied in a non-standard way), Midland General and Notts & Derby (blue/cream), and South Midland (maroon/cream). And of course Royal Blue coaches were dark blue/cream.

Of course in the early postwar years, Bristol and ECW were not exclusive suppliers to nationalised concerns. They had existing customers from the municipal and company sectors, and they were being encouraged to export, so they were winning business from overseas countries. As soon as nationalisation came along, they could accept no more 'outside' orders, but were able to satisfy existing orders.

Before the war Bristol had built production up to over 600 bus chassis a year, and the postwar demand was such that between 1946 and 1950 it built an average of nearly 800 chassis per year. During the same period ECW produced almost exactly the same average number of bodies per year, though by no means all ECW bodies were on Bristol chassis, or vice versa.

Bristol/ECW K and L types joined most Tilling fleets — but not all. Brighton, Hove & District was all double-deck for many years and never bought Ls, Cumberland had its Leylands, the Balfour Beatty companies had recently-delivered

►

The clean interior styling of the Lincolnshire dual-purpose LS on the right, showing the typical ECW window arrangements, the high-back seating and the parcel racks. *Ian Allan library*

▲

The clean lines of the ECW bus body on the Bristol LS are accentuated by the reversed cream/green livery on Lincolnshire No 2214 (MFU 408), a 1955 LS5G with 41-seat dual-purpose body, seen when new, before delivery. *Ian Allan library*

The Bristol/ECW Lodekka offered Tilling Group operators the best of both worlds, and though some continued to buy highbridge K types (and indeed in a few cases lowbridge K types) after the introduction of the Lodekka, it fast became familiar throughout group fleets. Hants & Dorset No 1375 (SRU 988), seen here in May 1966, is a typical earlier Lodekka, a 1956 LD6B with 60-seat body. *R. L. Wilson*

The longer rear entrance Lodekkas were rarer beasts. Red & White No L160 (VAX 508), a 1960 30ft long FL6G with 70-seat body, is seen in October 1966. *R. L. Wilson*

The classic and understated lines of the ECW body for the Bristol LS, on Eastern Counties No LS765 (SNG 765), an LS5G with only 32 seats, seen when new competing in the Clacton Coach Rally, predecessor of today's Brighton event.
Ian Allan library

▲ single-deckers and only Notts & Derby took Ks, and the Red & White companies had their Albions.

The natural successor to the K and L types was to have been the M type, and two chassis were displayed by Bristol at the 1948 Commercial Motor Show, the first since the war, and the last time Bristol or ECW would exhibit at a trade show until 1966.

These were improved versions of the existing chassis, but were apparently designed with export business in mind, and sported a broader version of the traditional Bristol radiator, and a chrome bumper bar. The specification was not dramatically different, but a synchromesh gearbox was fitted. There were single-deck MS and double-deck MD chassis, with Bristol and Gardner six-cylinder engines respectively, but a combination of Bristol's own innovative design work and external forces dictated that the M type would never see production, and the chassis were dismantled. The synchromesh gearbox disappeared along the line somewhere, and Bristol reverted to its sturdy crash box, doubtless to the dismay of many drivers.

Although Bristol/ECW products quickly became the Tilling Group standard, in the early postwar period there was so much

scrambling for new chassis that the group had to look beyond its own resources for supplies.

The most notable move to outside suppliers was the order for 100 Leyland Titan PD1A chassis which received ECW lowbridge bodies. These were delivered, in 1947, to Crosville, Eastern Counties, Eastern National, Hants & Dorset, Lincolnshire, Southern National and Western National. Later in the year 25 more PD1As were bought, fitted with ECW highbridge bodies, and delivered — ironically enough — to Bristol Tramways. There may have been some underlying motive here, for it would give the Bristol company first-hand experience of a successful open market chassis, and allow comparisons with its own products on similar routes. Something similar happened in 1963 when, following the takeover of the Silver Star business by Wilts & Dorset, three Leyland Atlanteans were diverted to join the Bristol fleet, where, it is suggested, they gave Bristol the opportunity to study the rear-engined double-decker, leading to its introduction of the VR chassis.

If the K type seemed solid and unexceptional, Bristol's next double-decker was anything but. The Tilling Group had a significant need for lowbridge double-deckers with a laden height of just 13ft 2in, which was 1ft lower than a highbridge K. Low railway bridges on interurban routes, and sometimes even garages and bus stations, dictated the need for lower buses, and between 1946 and 1957 ECW built six lowbridge bodies for every four highbridge. A bus that could offer the convenience of normal upper deck seating, with a centre gangway, in a bus that would pass under low bridges, was clearly the answer, but UK construction and use regulations specified minimum saloon heights, and this made the use of a normal chassis impossible.

Bristol's answer was to lower the floor line on the lower deck to permit this, and the prototype Lodekka, surely one of the most significant buses of the 20th century, was unveiled in 1949. The bus achieved its low height with a transmission layout that divided ahead of the rear axle, with propeller shafts running to worm drive units on each side of the rear axle. In essence this did away with the need for a normal rear axle, which could then be cranked down to allow a low-slung gangway. The chassis had a broad radiator similar to the M type prototypes, and a slightly uneasy-looking ECW body based on the contemporary highbridge design.

A second Lodekka prototype was completed in 1950, in the colours of the West Yorkshire company. It carried a body that was similar to the highbridge design on contemporary Bristol KSW chassis. The two prototypes were then used as demonstration vehicles, visiting Tilling and Scottish companies, allowing Tilling to gain operating experience and feedback from company engineering and traffic staff.

When pre-production Lodekkas followed in 1953 they had a revised transmission layout with a single propeller shaft, but a drop-centre rear axle, a Bristol development that went on to be adopted by other manufacturers looking for low-floor capability.

Full production of the Lodekka started in 1954, with LD6B, LD5G and LD6G variants produced. Like the six 1953 pre-production buses, these had a concealed radiator of the type that was fashionable in the early 1950s, with separate mudwings. The front incorporated a representation of the Bristol grille shape, initially containing thick radiator slats, but on production chassis the grille slats were much finer. The ECW body had deep windows on both decks, and the front end was pleasantly rounded. The inevitable difference in height between the engine compartment/driver's cab and the low-slung body was treated sympathetically, certainly rather better

than was the case on some later similar models from other manufacturers.

The K type continued to be offered alongside the LD, but between 1954 and 1957, when K series production ended, only 327 K types were built (all but 33 with highbridge bodies), compared with 1,466 LDs.

The single-deck successor to the Bristol L type was also to a very different layout, though less revolutionary than the Lodekka. The LS (Light Saloon) was, in the fashion of the day, a 30ft-long chassis with the engine mounted horizontally under the floor. The LS was strictly an underframe, designed to be integrated directly with the body which would, of course, be built by ECW. This semi-integral layout led to great structural rigidity, and saved weight. The prototype weighed 5 tons 12cwt, and while production LSs weighed over 6 tons, the low weight on what always appeared to be a substantial bus was praiseworthy. Although one of the prototypes, for Eastern Counties, had a Gardner 4HLW engine, production LSs were offered with Gardner 5HLW or 6HLW or Bristol LSW (a horizontal version of the AVW) engines.

There were LS buses and coaches, and ECW developed two main body styles for these. The bus had a plain front, initially

ECW built 16 unusual, but attractive, semi-chassisless buses for Eastern Counties in 1950 using units from prewar Gardner 4LK-engined Dennis Ace buses. One of these useful lightweight buses, No CD843 (HPW 828), in Peterborough in April 1954. *R. L. Wilson*

The Bristol SC4LK was ideal for narrow rural routes. Crosville No SSG650 (647 LFM), negotiates the hairpin bend at Lawnt, near Denbigh, in July 1965 on its Wednesday afternoon trip to Peniel. *A. Moyes*

Another of the rarer Lodekka variants was the FSF. This is Western National No 1012 (707 JHY), a 1960 FSF6G with 60-seat forward entrance ECW body, bought from Bristol Omnibus in 1967.
Arnold Richardson/Photobus

The Bristol/ECW LS model was a useful high-capacity bus. Wilts & Dorset No 520 (JAM 152), a 1952 LS6G with 41-seat dual purpose body, is seen in Salisbury bus station in August 1963 after it had been repainted in bus livery. *G. W. Dickson*

In its express guise, based on the bus bodyshell, Durham District No DBE19 (2919 HN), a Bristol MW5G with 41-seat body, at speed in July 1963. *R. L. Wilson*

The second style of ECW coach body for Bristol MW chassis was much improved by deeper front windscreens and a straight waistrail. United Counties No 261 (GRP 261D) was an MW6G 39-seater new in 1966, and is seen at Exeter in June 1966. *G. Mead*

with a rather heavy-looking three-part destination display, but was very obviously an ECW body. The coach was a splendidly understated design in an era of over-ornamentation, with a straight waistline, the minimum of extra brightwork, and a winged motif on the front panelling.

LS production started in 1952 and very soon the L type variants were regarded as outdated. In total, 1,392 LSs were bodied by ECW between 1950 (prototypes) and 1958; of these, 777 were buses, 421 coaches and 194 were classed as express types, basically bus shells with better seating, and added external embellishments.

As with the K type, L types were built alongside LSs but only in very limited numbers. ECW also rebodied older L type chassis, often to suit driver-only operation. The only LS types to carry non-ECW bodies were delivered to the Scottish Group's Western SMT company, which specified Alexander bodywork, as it would later do on Bristol MW chassis. As the Scottish Group was still able to buy 'outside' chassis and bodies, it bought mainstream buses, typically from AEC or Leyland with bodies by Alexander or Northern Counties, as well as Bristol/ECW products from 1954. It became a good Lodekka customer, but the only Bristol/ECW single-deckers it

bought were small batches of LS6G coaches and buses, and MW6G coaches. LS types were bought by most of the major Tilling operators.

With LS buses seating up to 45 passengers, Tilling recognised a need for a lighter, smaller-capacity bus for rural work. This materialised in 1954 as the SC type, designated SC4LK to signify its front-mounted 3.8-litre Gardner 4LK engine. The SC was built between 1954 and 1962, and 327 were built; of these 50 were fitted out as coaches. The SC4LK was delivered to Crosville, Cumberland, Eastern Counties, Eastern National, Lincolnshire, Red & White, Thames Valley, United Counties and United Welsh.

In 1955, Bristol was set up as a separate manufacturing company, and the title Bristol Commercial Vehicles was adopted.

When 30ft-long double-deckers were legalised from 1956, Bristol developed a 30ft Lodekka, coded LDL, and six prototypes were built in 1957. These were 70-seaters, compared with the 58 or 60 in most LDs. But there were other Lodekka changes which would further develop this revolutionary concept. Prototypes of the new design were built in 1958/9, featuring air suspension on the rear axle, giving a virtually flat lower saloon floor, and air-pressure, rather than vacuum, brakes. The two prototypes were designated LDS (27ft long) and LDL (30ft long), and there were eight further LDS types for the Brighton, Hove & District company.

Although the Lodekka layout had obvious attractions to companies outside the state sector, similar models developed by the mainstream chassis builders met with mixed success. AEC developed the Bridgemaster, followed by the Renown, and Leyland the Lowlander. Dennis bought the rights to manufacture the Lodekka under licence as the Loline, initially very much a Lodekka clone, but later incorporating more Dennis ideas.

Many operators were moving towards forward entrances on their front-engined double-deckers, so Bristol worked on such a model, which materialised as the prototype FLF Lodekka in 1959. The flat-floor Lodekkas now had F-series designations — FS for the 27ft rear entrance model, FSF for its forward entrance variant, FL for the 30ft-long version of the FS, and FLF for the 30ft forward entrance bus. After the original LD type (2,180 built), the FLF was the most popular Lodekka variant, with sales of 1,867. The FS type sold nearly 900, but the FL and FSF types were less popular, with sales of 45 and 218 respectively.

There were even some extra long (31ft) FLFs built in 1966-8 for Scottish Group companies, and for Eastern National, with seats for up to 78 passengers. The Bristol engine offered for the Lodekka was, from 1958, the 8.9-litre BVW unit. Gardner's more powerful 10.45-litre 6LX was a popular choice, and the 9.8-litre Leyland O.600 was available in later FLFs, as was semi-automatic transmission.

More than 5,200 Lodekkas were built between 1949 and 1968 and every major Tilling bus company received examples.

The LS single-decker was replaced in 1957 by a new model, the MW (Medium Weight), which was a conventional underfloor-engined chassis. ECW developed new bus and coach bodies for the MW, and these were broadly similar to the bodies on LS, but with low-mounted grilles on the front, and a rather more relaxed front profile on the bus. The MW was only available with Gardner 5HLW (MW5G) or 6HLW (MW6G) engines. In practice, as with the LS, many fleets with less demanding territory found the 5HLW more than adequate, with the 6HLW specified for difficult territory or for coach work. In 1961 a new coach body style was introduced for the MW. As is often the case with bodybuilders that concentrate

on service buses, it still had a bus-like appearance, but with a rather fussy front end and an oddly-stepped waistline. Later versions were improved with deeper front windscreens and a straight waistline. The MW was delivered to every major Tilling company, except Brighton, Hove & District.

To replace the SC rural bus, Bristol/ECW introduced the SU (Small Underfloor), a small underfloor-engined chassis with a four-cylinder Albion EN250 engine. Albion had fitted this engine in its small Nimbus model in 1955, and the Bristol chassis were the SUS (24ft 4in long) and SUL (28ft long); in each case the suffix '4A' was added to the designation. The bodywork was typically ECW, but with a high-mounted front radiator grille and shallow windscreens. The SU was in production between 1959 and 1966, and 181 were built, all but 50 being SUL models, and the great majority of these being buses. Tilling fleets choosing the SU were Bristol, Southern Vectis, United Auto, United Counties, United Welsh, West Yorkshire and Western/Southern National.

When the overall length of UK buses was relaxed to 36ft in 1961, the major 'outside' chassis manufacturers, AEC and Leyland, chose to lengthen their existing underfloor-engined Reliance and Leopard chassis. Bristol could have produced a

▲ Photographed while on loan to Hants & Dorset in February 1951, the trend-setting 1949 Bristol Lodekka LDX prototype, Bristol Tramways No C5000 (LHY 949) with ECW 58-seat body, alongside Hants & Dorset No 1247 (JEL 266), a Bristol K5G with lowbridge ECW 55-seat body, also new in 1949. *Ian Allan library*

The Bristol/ECW SC type was an economical rural bus, and although it is most readily associated with Tilling fleets in the southern half of the country, it was also bought by Cumberland. No 202 (VAO 391), is a 1958 SC4LK with 35-seat ECW bus body. *Arnold Richardson/Photobus*

Three United Auto Bristol/ECW MW types with similar bodies, but fitted out and liveried for different duties. From left to right are No UE583 (2583 HN), a 1960 MW5G with 41-seat dual-purpose seats, in dual-purpose livery; U537 (937 JHN), a 1958 MW5G 41-seat bus, in bus livery; and UE708 (908 THN), a 1963 MW6G with 39-seat dual-purpose body in Tyne-Tees-Thames coach livery. They were photographed in August 1967. *R. L. Wilson*

An example of the later style of ECW coach body on Bristol MW chassis, with deeper front screens and a straight waistline, Crosville No CMG36 (OFM 36E), a MW6G 39-seater new in 1967. *Policy Transport Photographs*

▶ Inside the lower saloon, looking towards the rear entrance, of Bristol Tramways No C5000, the prototype Lodekka, showing the flat gangway leading straight on to the platform. *Ian Allan library*

▲ The bare bones of a Lodekka show the admirably low chassis frame. This is an FSF model, that will receive a 27ft-long ECW forward entrance body. *Ian Allan library*

◀ The rare 30ft-long FL type Bristol Lodekka, represented by Hants & Dorset No 1485 (7685 LJ), a 1962 FL6G with 70-seat ECW body, turning into Bridge Street, Christchurch in June 1964. Note the extra window bay, and the emergency exit behind the driver's cab. *W. T. Cansick*

36ft MW (though some 31ft-long MW coaches were produced), but chose instead to develop a totally new model, the RE (Rear Engine). This used a horizontal 10.45-litre Gardner 6HLX engine mounted under the floor behind the rear axle. Initial models were of the RELL (Long Low-frame) and RELH (Long High-frame) types, for bus and coach bodies respectively. The ECW bus body was clearly a Lowestoft product, but featured an attractively styled front end with curved glass screens. The bus body went on to receive a rather less attractive flat front, with shallow screens, then a version with deeper screens, and then, from 1970, the version with BET-style curved screens, regarded by many as the classic RE.

The coach body was based on the revised MW design, and in the production version this was greatly improved with panoramic side windows.

In 1965 a share exchange with Leyland, a consequence of Leyland's close links with government, meant that Bristol and ECW products, together and separately, could be sold on the open market for the first time since 1948. ECW bodies were quickly specified on a variety of chassis, and the Bristol RE became a popular choice with municipal and BET fleets. New versions of the RE appeared in 1966, the RESL bus and RESH coach, suitable for bodies around 32ft long.

Bristol was aware that its only double-deck model, the

KEIGHLEY 26

PAY AS YOU ENTER

KEIGHLEY-WEST YORKSHIRE

807 BWR

The successor to the SC for lighter duties was the Bristol/ECW SU, available in short and long version. This longer SUL4A 36-seat bus is Keighley-West Yorkshire No KSMA1 (807 BWR), a 1962 example, seen in Keighley. *G. W. Dickson*

Deliveries of the Bristol RELL were well underway when the Tilling Group passed into the new National Bus Company in 1969. This 1968 Crosville example, No SRG46 (UFM 46F) is a RELL6G with ECW 53-seat body, seen in June 1968 at Woodside Ferry, Birkenhead. *R. L. Wilson*

The only English customer for the extra-long 31ft Lodekka was Eastern National. The extra length of No 2930 (AVW 399F), a 1967 70-seat FLF6G, is seen in 1968. *W. T. Cansick*

▲ Lodekka — however reliable — was looking dated alongside the Daimler Fleetlines and Leyland Atlanteans being placed in service by BET, municipal and independent fleets, and with the possibility of driver-only operation spreading to double-deck buses, a new model was clearly necessary.

Before this could be launched, however, Bristol announced its intention to produce a Lodekka model with a conventional chassis frame; the F series models had a chassis frame that was designed to be married to the ECW bodywork for structural strength. A new chassis, the LDL, was to be built with full-depth side-members, which would have involved an increase in overall body height — to 14ft 1in, it was estimated, though it was suggested that 13ft 9in was possible with suitable body design. The chassis was to be available with Gardner 6LX or Leyland O.600 engines, and the Bristol constant-mesh gearbox was to be standard.

This was rather a late attempt to break into a market that was already over-provided, and none of the new LDL models was ever built.

This would have been a stopgap, because Bristol was working on a new generation of rear-engined chassis which would be suitable for double-deck or single-deck use. The N type (following on from the 1948 M type) would have a vertical engine mounted in-line at the rear offside of the chassis. There were to be ND type double-deckers (36ft NDL, 32ft 6in NDS) and NS single-deckers (low-floor bus or high-floor coach, 36ft long). In practice, the single-deck N types never materialised, as Bristol continued with the highly successful RE; the ND type became the VR (Vertical Rear), and the first examples appeared late in 1966, with attractive 80-seat bodies by ECW. They were strictly VRLS (VR longtitudinal short), and were the only versions built to this specification. The two buses, coded VRX by Bristol, were demonstrators, one in Bristol Omnibus green, the other in Central SMT red.

Although Ribble chose the VRLL for its notorious 36ft-long ECW-bodied motorway coaches, and VRLs were built for South African customers, it was clear that UK operators were looking for a bus around 30ft long, and with a transversely rear-mounted engine, as in the Atlantean and Fleetline. Government plans to help bus operators restock their fleets with new buses suitable for driver-only operation, by offering a 25% grant towards the costs (later increasing to 50%) led Bristol to rush to get a new model into production. This was the VRT (Vertical Rear Transverse), and the first examples were delivered late in 1968, without the usual Bristol development period, and the use of prototypes as in-service demonstrators. The result, sadly, was that the new VRT was not really ready, and it took some time to get the model right.

Only a dozen ECW-bodied VRTs had entered service with Tilling Group companies by 31 December 1968, when the group ceased to exist, with the new National Bus Company taking over the following day. These went to Eastern National, Thames Valley and Western National (one each), and West Yorkshire (nine).

The only other Bristol model introduced during the Tilling Group years was a lightweight underfloor-engined single-decker, the LH (Light Horizontal). This used the 5.8-litre Perkins H6.354 or 6.54-litre Leyland O.400 engines, and was available in LHS (26ft long), LH (30ft) or LHL (36ft) forms. It was essentially a replacement for the Bristol SU range,

together with Leyland's Tiger Cub. In the absence of a suitable lightweight bus, between the SU and LH, Eastern Counties, West Yorkshire and Western National had taken Bedford VAM chassis with ECW bodywork. Small numbers of LH buses, with ECW bodies, entered service with Tilling companies before the formation of NBC.

Duple-bodied Bedfords had been chosen by various Tilling fleets over the years for less demanding coach duties, and these had joined the Crosville, Cumberland, Eastern Counties, Eastern National, Lincolnshire, Mansfield District, South Midland, Southern Vectis, Thames Valley, Tillings, Western/Southern National and Wilts & Dorset fleets.

From the situation it inherited in 1948, with a very mixed fleet of vehicles, the Tilling Group had introduced a remarkably high level of standardisation in its fleets, with the L, LS, SC, MW, RE and SU single-deckers, and the K and Lodekka double-deckers, virtually all of them with standard ECW bodies. The BET Group never attempted to impose these levels of standardisation on its members, and adopted a less centralist role.

The results of Tilling's policies were there to see: the economy of standardisation, the supply of buses suited to the group's operating areas, from lightweights for rural work, to coaches for express and touring work, buses for long interurban duties and for intensive urban operation. The buses built by Bristol and ECW were attractive and practical, if not always at the cutting edge of body design, and they were very fuel-efficient — though perhaps hard work for drivers with those crash gearboxes. Overall, Tilling's standardisation policies seem to have paid off handsomely, and inevitably contributed to the smooth running and profitability of the group companies.

The RELH6G was a worthy successor to previous generations of Bristol coaches on the Royal Blue express services operated by Southern National and Western National. No 2363 (ATA 105B) of 1964 in the Southern National fleet, with 45-seat ECW body, at Victoria Coach Station, London.
Arnold Richardson/Photobus

The clean lines of the ECW coach body for the Bristol RELH are accentuated in this June 1964 view of new Eastern National No 579 (AVX 962B), an RELH6G with 42-seat body, at Lincoln. *G. W. Dickson*

Right at the end of the Tilling years came the Bristol LH, a lightweight underfloor-engined chassis. Western National No 713 (MUO 325F) is a 1968 LH6L with 41-seat ECW body. Alongside is No 707 (KDV 137F), a Bedford VAM5 with 41-seat ECW body, a rare combination, bought for similar duties in the West Country.
Arnold Richardson/Photobus

The ECW coach body for the high-frame Bristol RELH was rather less satisfactory, with shallow windscreens and a rather bus-like Bristol grille. The lines were otherwise simple and effective, with interesting curved rear glasses. Crosville No CRG525 (7286 FM), an RELH6G 47-seater, is seen in West Kirby in July 1968. *R. L. Wilson*

Several Tilling fleets chose Bedford/Duple coaches for tour, excursion and hire work. Southern Vectis No 240 (SDL 4), at Alum Bay in June 1966, is a 1959 SB8 with 41-seat coachwork. *R. L. Wilson*

Unusual Tilling purchases at a time of high demand for new buses were the Leyland Titan PD1As which received ECW bodies. Eastern National No 1114 (MPU 44) was a 1947 lowbridge 53-seater, seen in April 1960 at Leigh Beck. *G. Mead*

Bedford coaches were bought by several Tilling fleets for private hire and lighter coaching work. Midland General MC25 (TRB 582F) is a 1968 VAM5 with Duple Viceroy 45-seat coachwork. *Policy Transport Photographs*

Acquisitions of private operators brought variety into several Tilling fleets. Looking out of place in Tilling red is Wilts & Dorset No 995 (PMW 386), a 1957 Leyland Tiger Cub PSUC1/2 with 41-seat Harrington body, bought in 1963 with the business of Silver Star, Porton Down. *Arnold Richardson/Photobus*

A taste of things to come was given by the appearance late in 1968 of the only 12 Bristol VRTs to be delivered to Tilling Group fleets before the new National Bus Company took over on 1 January 1969. Western National received one of these buses, and No 1059 (OTA 293G) from the same batch, actually delivered early in 1969, is seen working on Plymouth joint services on Easter Sunday 1969. It is a VRT/SL6G with 70-seat ECW body.
D. Withers

▲ 5. The Tilling Legacy

The story of the Tilling Group really ended with the formation of the National Bus Company on 1 January 1969, but its legacy continued for many years in the operating methods and vehicles of the former group companies. Welding together Tilling and BET, with their very different areas and their very different approaches to running large groups, was not an easy task, and the directors of NBC soon realised that the old structure, which only made sense when the two groups were under different ownership, had to be altered to rationalise operations around the country.

This inevitably led to the disappearance of familiar names among both camps. On the Tilling side, Brighton, Hove & District disappeared into Southdown, Crosville gained part of North Western after that company was split up, Hants & Dorset and Wilts & Dorset were merged, Mansfield District moved to East Midland, Midland General/Notts & Derby were merged into Trent, Red & White became part of National Welsh, South Midland went to City of Oxford, Thames Valley

merged with Aldershot & District to become Alder Valley, Tillings disappeared into National Travel South East, United Welsh went to South Wales, and Western National finally absorbed Southern National and gained Devon General. Bristol, Cumberland, Eastern Counties, Eastern National, Lincolnshire, United Auto, United Counties and West Yorkshire stayed much as they had been.

Some of the old names reappeared, firstly as part of the Market Analysis Project, and later following privatisation in the 1980s, and there are many companies, most today under the control of one of the mega-groups, that are still very recognisably the companies developed and nurtured by the Tilling Group.

Annual reports are normally fairly unexciting reading, including only those details that are legally and tactically necessary. But the final report of the Transport Holding Co, covering the year 1968, offers 'A Retrospect', which provides an illuminating and remarkably frank look at the years of state ownership.

The retrospect covers the 21 years of public ownership since 1948, and points out that approximately 13 years of these 21 'were spent waiting for major Transport Acts of Parliament, whether good or not-so-good, and in reorganising after them'. The (anonymous) writer recalls that the years 1948 and 1949 were occupied with the vast job of acquisition and rationalisation, that the years 1952-4 were spent either in 'a state of deep-freeze prior to the Act of 1953 or cleaning up subsequently', that the next period of 'organisational and development stasis occurred over the four years prior to the Act of 1962' and that finally there was the period 1966-8, preparing for the final chapter of THC.

'In addition to the consequences of constant legislation or its equivalent', the writer continues, 'there has also been, of course, the burden of considerable political intervention.' The level of interference had, it seems, increased over the years.

Much of the early attention, while still under BTC control, focused on the railways, and early BTC Annual Reports dwell at great length on the problems of the railways, and the activities of the (highly profitable) bus companies are largely just nodded through. As government paid closer and closer attention to the fate of the railways, the bus and other interests became implicated.

As far as the short life of the THC is concerned, the writer notes that THC had earned £90 million in the six years of its

The peculiar Alder Valley fleet-name appeared on former Aldershot & District and Thames Valley buses, in full NBC corporate style, as on former Thames Valley No 535 (MBL 843), an elderly Bristol/ECW LD6G 60-seater, new in 1956. *Michael Dryhurst*

existence. 'But it was strong enough, in its constitution and in its own attitudes, and was encouraged to enjoy a reasonable degree of freedom — at least until the last year or two. And with a still greater degree of freedom the profits for the six years would have been greater than £90 million. Nor, it is thought, would the customers of the public interest have suffered.'

The 1968 Report is quick to point out that THC was not a nationalised industry; this, it says, implies the monopoly of a complete field. It prefers the term 'public corporation', which is subject to the same legal requirements as private companies in the same sector.

The writer argues for 'controlled degrees' of cross-subsidy to allow commercial services to assist social ones, but this was an argument the bus industry would eventually lose in the Thatcher years.

No punches are pulled in the conclusion of this retrospect. 'Doubtless it is difficult for those not immediately concerned to appreciate that the price paid for uncompromising and political involvement is not simply some minor and incidental damage to the undertaking, far outweighed by the benefits to be expected from the public discussions and decisions which result, and capable of being rapidly repaired. The consequences reach to the very core of the undertaking in due course.'

Annual reports must finish on a positive note, and the writer concludes: 'the Holding Company has no doubt that men [sic] of the right kind will continue to be attracted to the vitally important and challenging world of public transport; and that there need be no reason to doubt the future success of the bodies which now follow the Holding Company.'

Nobody in 1968 could have anticipated the changes that totally altered the structure and ownership of the bus industry in the 1980s, but the THC, and the BTC before it, had every reason to be proud of its record as controllers of a large portion of Britain's bus industry.

After operating an all-double-deck fleet for many years, Brighton Hove & District succumbed to single-deckers in 1968 when it bought Bristol RESL6Gs with two-door ECW 35-seat bodies. After Southdown takeover, No 2209 (PPM 209G) is seen at the Old Steine, Brighton. *Roy Marshall/Photobus*

Old-timers lingered on into National Bus Company days, like Southern Vectis No 909 (FRU 303), a 1944 Bristol K5G with rebuilt Strachans 59-seat body, acquired from Hants & Dorset and seen in July 1971. *Dave Brown*

The shorter-length Bristol
RESL model was due to
appear in National Bus
Company fleets, but a few
entered service during
Tilling Group days,
including Crosville
No ERG1 (OFM 1E), an
RESL6G with 42-seat ECW
dual-purpose body, seen in
Delamere Street, Chester, in
July 1967. *R. L. Wilson*

The Brighton, Hove &
District name, and distinctive
red/cream livery lasted for a
while on Southdown buses
after the two fleets were
merged under NBC. No 2113
(VUF 313K), a 1971
Daimler Fleetline CRL6 with
dual-door 71-seat Northern
Counties body, is seen in
Brighton.
Michael Dryhurst

◄ The death-knell for full-size Bristol single-deckers was sounded by another product from within the Leyland group, the integral Leyland National, which quickly became familiar throughout NBC territory, even where a less urban bus might have been more suitable. Ironically, this posed view shows No C1406 (JHU 847L), a 1972 model 1151/2R 44-seat two-door version delivered to the Bristol Omnibus fleet. *Ian Allan library*

Further Reading

The importance of the Tilling Group to the history of the British bus industry is reflected in the many books that cover aspects of its operations. The books I found particularly valuable in researching this title were: *A National Bus Company Album* by Ray Stenning (Viewfinder, 1979); *Bristol VR* by Martin S. Curtis (Ian Allan, 1994); *British Buses Before 1945* by John Aldridge (Ian Allan, 1995); *British Buses Since 1945* by Stephen Morris (Ian Allan, 1995); *Bus Operators: 2 — NBC, Antecedents & Formation* by Stewart J. Brown (Ian Allan, 1983); *Eastern Coach Works 1946-1965* by Maurice Doggett and Alan Townsin (Venture Publications, 1993);

Eastern Coach Works 1965-1987 by Maurice Doggett and Alan Townsin (Venture Publications, 1994); *Golden Age of Buses* by Charles F. Klapper (Routledge & Kegan Paul, 1978); *The Bristol Story, Part One — 1908-1951* by Alan Townsin (Venture Publications, 1996); *The History of British Bus Services* by John Hibbs (David & Charles, 1968); *The Official ABC Coach Guide for Great Britain*, and *The Years before National* by Ray Stenning (Fleetline Books, 1982). There are also a number of histories of individual Tilling Group companies, mostly published by Venture and its predecessor, Transport Publishing Company. Although a number of these books are out of print, they may be found at rallies and other enthusiast events, or from specialist dealers. I also made use of BTC and THC Annual Reports for the years from 1948 to 1968.

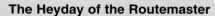